A STRAIGHTFORWARD

GUIDE TO TEACHER MERIT PAY

"As a former middle school principal and school superintendent, I have had 20 years of experience with performance pay in the state of Arizona. I wish I had read this book before embarking on my performance pay journey. The timelines for program development and implementation are exactly the steps I would follow if I were to begin my journey again. Congratulations to the authors for writing such an outstanding text to help the school leaders of the present and future."

—*L. Thomas Heck, Clinical Associate Professor, Arizona State University, and former Superintendent, Litchfield Elementary District, Arizona*

"*A Straightforward Guide to Teacher Merit Pay* is your one-stop resource for understanding the history, research, and implementation tools for establishing a merit pay program in your school or district."

—*James Drexler, Dean of Education, Covenant College*

"Performance pay for teaching has increasingly become part of the national education agenda to improve teacher quality and student outcomes. As a result, more and more states, districts, and schools are making performance pay a cornerstone of their strategy to revolutionize the way teachers are trained, supported, evaluated, and compensated. This guide is a useful resource for undertaking merit pay, preventing pitfalls, and most important, creating a well-designed roadmap."

—*Gary Stark, President/CEO, National Institute for Excellence in Teaching, University of Arkansas*

"*A Straightforward Guide to Teacher Merit Pay* presents a thoughtfully crafted and research-based investigation of how merit pay can work in a school system. For policymakers and practitioners alike, these principles for developing a merit plan should reframe the merit pay debate. Moreover, school leaders will resonate with how skillfully the authors have bridged theory and practice in a practical guide to proposing and implementing a merit-based pay system."

—*John C. Pijanowski, Associate Professor of Educational Leadership, University of Arkansas*

"Gary Ritter and Joshua Barnett give a great overview of the history and positive and negative aspects of merit pay. They reveal the advantages of developing such a program for a school."

—*Gary Lee Frye, Homeless Liaison/Grant Writer, Lubbock-Cooper ISD, Texas*

"*A Straightforward Guide to Teacher Merit Pay* examines the research and history on merit pay, which is quite enlightening to those with limited prior knowledge of the topic. The practical recommendations are grounded in common sense and experience. Decision makers will be delighted with the authors' treatment of this topic."

—*Jude A. Huntz, Chancellor, Catholic Diocese of Kansas City*

"Gary Ritter and Joshua Barnett have captured extensive historical background information to provide a context for present day public schools. *A Straightforward Guide to Teacher Merit Pay* has helped me process my reflections on four decades in the profession."

—*Douglas Gordon Hesbol, Educational Consultant and Retired Superintendent, Yorkville, Illinois*

"*A Straightforward Guide to Teacher Merit Pay* is a great handbook for anyone wanting to learn about merit pay plans and considering how to get such a process started. It is easy to read and contains lots of examples and ideas based on the experience of the authors."

—*Gloria L. Johnston, Retired Superintendent*

A STRAIGHTFORWARD
GUIDE TO TEACHER MERIT PAY

Encouraging and Rewarding Schoolwide Improvement

GARY W. RITTER
JOSHUA H. BARNETT

FOREWORD BY JAMES GUTHRIE

CORWIN
A SAGE Company

CORWIN
A SAGE Company

FOR INFORMATION:

Corwin

A SAGE Company

2455 Teller Road

Thousand Oaks, California 91320

www.corwin.com

SAGE Ltd.

1 Oliver's Yard

55 City Road

London, EC1Y 1SP

United Kingdom

SAGE Pvt. Ltd.

B 1/I 1 Mohan Cooperative Industrial Area

Mathura Road, New Delhi 110 044

India

SAGE Publications Asia-Pacific Pte. Ltd.

3 Church Street

#10–04 Samsung Hub

Singapore 049483

Acquisitions Editor: Arnis Burvikovs

Associate Editor: Desirée A. Bartlett

Editorial Assistant: Mayan White

Permissions Editor: Jennifer Barron

Project Editor: Veronica Stapleton

Copy Editor: Megan Granger

Typesetter: Hurix Systems Pvt. Ltd.

Proofreader: Dennis W. Webb

Indexer: Jean Casalegno

Cover Designer: Edgar Abarca

Printed in the United States of America

Library of Congress Cataloging-in-Publication Data

Ritter, Gary W.
A straightforward guide to teacher merit pay: encouraging and rewarding schoolwide improvement / Gary W. Ritter, Joshua H. Barnett; foreword by James Guthrie.

pages cm

Includes bibliographical references and index.

ISBN 978-1-4522-5551-4 (pbk.)

1. Teachers—Salaries, etc.—United States. 2. Merit pay—United States. 3. School improvement programs—United States. I. Title.

LB2842.22.R58 2013

371.1—dc23

2013005339

This book is printed on acid-free paper.

13 14 15 16 17 10 9 8 7 6 5 4 3 2 1

Contents

Foreword

Gary Ritter and Joshua Barnett have written a timely and practical book.

The magnitude and cost of the education workforce—to say nothing of the importance of the function performed by professional educators—screams for better ways to attract, evaluate, motivate, and reward talent. This book addresses many related questions and provides many appropriate answers.

The United States employs about 4 million professional educators annually. This is a figure virtually equal to the total number of federal government employees.

This workforce, considering both its pay and benefits, costs around $400 billion each year, a figure that approximates the budget for the U.S. Department of Defense.

These figures alone justify careful scrutiny of the means by which professional educators are evaluated and paid. When information is added regarding the significance of effective teachers in the role of facilitating student learning, then a reader can further understand the timeliness and utility of this book.

Erick Hanushek's and Steve Rivkin's research on teachers' effectiveness provides crucial additional information. Thanks to their empirical results, we can now verify our commonsense understanding that teachers are the most powerful engine we have in the education arsenal. An effective teacher trumps class size, facilities, technology, textbooks, and a string of other school-related resources when it comes to contributing to academic achievement.

A student sufficiently fortunate to have effective teachers 3 years in a row is virtually guaranteed to be proficient in reading, the key to further lifelong learning. If every minority student in the nation had effective teachers in his or her elementary years, we would come near to closing the achievement gap between advantaged and disadvantaged students.

Regrettably, the obverse is also accurate. An ineffective teacher actively imperils the prospect of student learning. A student so unfortunate as to have ineffective elementary school teachers several years in a row is at risk of never being able to perform at grade level in reading and mathematics.

These figures and findings make clear the significance to the nation and its children of having effective teachers. Regrettably, evidence regarding the quality of the educator workforce suggests that the United States is headed in the opposite direction. In contrast to the immediate pre– and post–World War II era, when women were restricted in their career choices relative to today, schools can no longer be assured of drawing their teachers from the top quartiles of talent. Teaching is simply not as attractive a profession as it was half a century ago.

All factors considered—the magnitude and cost of the workforce, the significance of teachers in the learning lives of students, and the need to restore teaching as an occupation worthy of even talented individuals—it is crucial to rethink the means for evaluating and rewarding educators.

However, the challenge is daunting. There are major technical and political hurdles to assessing and rewarding effective teaching.

What criteria are to be used to determine professional effectiveness? How does one fairly control for the talent and motivation of a teacher's students. What levels of annual pay would induce even more qualified individuals to seek teaching as a career? Who should evaluate the performance of teachers?

There are many more related questions, both of a policy and practical nature. The good news is that there is a mounting body of empirical evidence to serve as a basis for providing answers.

Ritter and Barnett have assembled the evidence and, in an even-handed and useful manner, have distilled answers.

It is their comprehensive approach and practicality that commends this book to policymakers and school and teacher leaders.

—*James W. Guthrie, Superintendent of Public Instruction,*
State of Nevada

Preface

In U.S. education policy, reform trends cycle in and back out of the spotlight. One such reform is merit pay for educators, which has recently reemerged at the top of the education policy agenda and in the public eye. In his first major education policy speech, President Obama promoted merit pay for teachers, and the Obama Administration has regularly supported strategies consistent with teacher pay reform. Specifically, in the Race to the Top competition (2009), $4.4 billion in federal funds was made available to state departments of education for development of policies encouraging school leaders to base teacher evaluations, and even pay, on students' performance on standardized assessments. Moreover, the Obama Administration expanded the Teacher Incentive Fund program, which was created during the Bush Administration in 2006 by the U.S. Department of Education as a competitive grant program for states and districts to develop incentive pay systems for educators. The Teacher Incentive Fund program under President Obama has allocated roughly another $1 billion in federal funds toward changing educator salaries. At the same time, prominent local and state merit pay programs, such as those in Denver, Florida, and Texas, have driven momentum and dollars toward developing alternative strategies for teacher compensation.

Indeed, the question of teacher compensation may be the most controversial in the already heated world of education reform. Of course, any issue that involves pay and job security for some 3.5 million teachers across the country is bound to be a politically sensitive one. Furthermore, the debate revolves around the fundamental question of whether "more effective" teachers should reap greater rewards than do their "less effective" peers. Implicit in this discussion is the assumption that some teachers are less effective than others. While most of us would acknowledge that, in any field, some people are more effective than others, this conversation is complicated by the fact that all these teachers are working with our nation's youngsters each year. And who among us would want to have his or her child assigned to the classroom of a less effective teacher? (Similarly, who among us would willingly choose to board a plane guided by a "less effective" pilot?) Our point here is simple: Despite the fact that there most certainly are more effective and less effective teachers, these are uncomfortable and controversial topics.

The controversy is further stoked by the uncertainty surrounding the statistical methods by which teacher effectiveness is measured. Indeed, there is hotly contested debate over the usefulness of so-called value-added models developed to estimate the influence of a teacher or a school on a student's academic growth over time. Some would argue that the imperfections of value-added models—or any models that attempt to ascertain teacher effectiveness based on student performance—are such that these models should play no role in the evaluation of teachers (Rothstein et al., 2010). The all-star list of authors of this Economic Policy Institute (EPI) brief included numerous preeminent scholars on teacher quality and educational assessment. However, a few months after the publication of the EPI research brief, another set of esteemed education researchers at the Brown Center on Education Policy at Brookings published what was, essentially, a rebuttal titled *Evaluating Teachers: The Important Role of Value-Added* (Glazerman et al., 2010). The Brookings team acknowledges that value-added measures are indeed estimates of teacher effectiveness and thus contain a level of measurement error. They conclude, however, that the measures need not be perfect to be useful. Ignoring the information provided in value-added models, they argue, does no good.

Unfortunately, while this debate rages in the academy, actual school leaders and practitioners operate in real time and are charged with the task of developing and implementing policies aimed toward placing the most effective educators (however measured) in front of students each and every day. Thus, while academics bicker and debate, administrators and educators are forced to try to sort through the milieu as policies are passed that encourage or require them to consider performance pay. This book is for those state, district, and school leaders who are curious about and interested in how a performance pay plan can be developed.

INTENDED AUDIENCE

Despite controversy over the theory behind merit pay and mixed evidence on the impact of such programs, school policymakers from around the country—and around the globe, for that matter—are giving serious consideration to this reform strategy. And, while there are a few books focused on the emerging scholarly research surrounding this question, as well as articles on the controversy over the intricacies and mathematical properties of teacher value-added models (see Berliner, 2014; Harris, 2011) used to measure teachers' impact on student learning, it is not clear where an administrator would go to seek practical guidance on how to consider the pros and cons and the details of implementing a merit pay plan in his or her district. To clarify, the academic conversation over value-added and merit pay will continue, but school leaders need a concise, straightforward explanation of what is known to help guide them in their decision making today. In the pages that follow, we hope to provide such a guide.

Specifically, our book is intended to provide information for school leaders who are curious about the possibilities of merit pay or to superintendents who will be implementing a plan but are not sure where to start. While we believe that a thoughtfully developed and carefully implemented merit pay plan can represent a positive policy alternative to the current system, this book is not intended to persuade individuals who are against merit pay. Rather, this book is intended to be a resource for those working with and in schools and school districts in which a merit pay plan is under consideration or in the development stages. This book provides a "how-to" guide to creating a potentially successful merit pay program that avoids some of the most common pitfalls.

OBJECTIVES/PURPOSE

In the first half of the book, we focus on the current landscape regarding merit pay in U.S. schools. In Chapters 1 through 4, we describe "what is" rather than "what should be." We conclude the first half of the book with a list of 12 standard criticisms of merit pay proposals, setting the table for how we might build effective plans. In the second half of the book, Chapters 5 through 8, we derive lessons from "what is" so we can imagine the characteristics of a merit pay plan with promise. In these chapters, we develop strategies and present recommendations for school leaders/administrators who might be considering the use of merit pay in their schools or districts.

The purpose of this book is threefold. First, we provide a holistic review of policies and evidence relating to merit pay programs. Second, we turn our attention to why merit pay can be a viable alternative to the current single-salary system and how to facilitate constructive conversations with those who are both opponents and supporters of merit pay programs. Third, we provide a detailed discussion of how to design, implement, and evaluate a merit-based program.

SPECIAL FEATURES

Our intention for this book is that it serve as a guide and resource, and we include a variety of suggestions and recommendations throughout to help practitioners and administrators considering a reform to the single-salary system. Specifically, the book contains five key features that we believe will be helpful resources for school leaders considering the use of an alternative pay scheme for teachers:

- *Twelve Key Responses to Criticisms of Merit Pay.* Chapter 4 describes the most common arguments against merit pay programs and provides a rationale and explanation—based on our extensive experience in working with educators, administrators, and policymakers—to help advance the conversation beyond "kneejerk" rejection.
- *Six Principles for Reforming Compensation Programs.* One of the most challenging aspects of considering how to change the compensation structure for educators is determining what needs to change and what it should be changed to. In essence, what works better? We walk through six guiding principles and why they are important in the process of reforming salaries.
- *Ten-Step Implementation Timeline.* One of the most daunting tasks of transforming the compensation structure in a school system is how and when to work through the process. We have developed our process through numerous programs and evaluations working with school districts.
- *"Invented" Exemplary Program.* Based on our experiences of working with several school districts in different states (in urban, suburban, rural, and tribal districts, and in union and non-union areas), we describe how to go from consideration to implementation through evaluation. Rather than present information from a particular program (actual programs are described in the literature area), we construct an illustrative program within a model school district and walk through the process.
- *Sample Materials.* With the intent of providing an effective "how-to" guide, we describe the steps of designing the program within the fictional district, and we provide actual, real materials we have used throughout our experiences. We have constructed a variety of tools, including teacher report cards, teacher surveys, and other tools provided in the appendices and described in Chapter 7.

Acknowledgments

We would like to acknowledge the many people who have encouraged and supported us throughout the writing of this book. As we have worked with school leaders to build innovative programs aimed at rewarding excellent educators, we have learned a great deal from colleagues and friends over small conversations in the hallways and much longer meetings away at conferences. We have developed our understanding in large part from reading, listening, and working with a host of individuals who also are working each day to build and evaluate potentially productive school improvement strategies of all sorts. Through these interactions, we have gained helpful insights into developing and implementing compensation reform strategies, and we have been reminded of the earnest need for providing better rewards to teachers. This book is a culmination of those experiences and those conversations, and for them, we are grateful.

We would like to provide some special thanks to members of several projects who helped get us moving on this path and helped keep us going. Nathan Jensen served as a key member on a variety of projects over the years, several of which are ongoing; his friendship and work continue to be invaluable. We would also like to acknowledge several other researchers and colleagues who have been instrumental to us in our exploration of the important and interesting issue of teacher pay. In particular, we are thankful for our partnerships and friendships with Jay Greene, Marc Holley, Marcus Winters, Lynn Woodworth, Roy Brooks, and Scott Ridley.

We are, of course, grateful to our team at Corwin Press, including Arnis Burvikovs, Desiree Bartlett, Veronica Hooper, and Megan Granger. Indeed, Arnis served as the initial catalyst for the project, and the consistent support, guidance, and encouragement provided by this group has allowed this book to come to fruition. Thank you for your tireless efforts to help keep us on track and guide us to the finish.

We are also deeply indebted to the teachers and school leaders with whom we have worked, who have challenged us to refine our own thinking and develop better plans. Most important, working alongside excellent school leaders and educators has served as a continuous reminder of the need for developing effective compensation models that encourage great educators to keep up the excellent work. Their support and willingness to try different ideas has greatly sharpened our arguments and understanding.

Finally, throughout this and all our work, we are greatly blessed to have the support of loving and giving families. We can't ever say thank you enough for the encouragement, guidance, and thoughtfulness provided to us, but we certainly know we wouldn't be able to accomplish much without you. Gary would like to recognize his parents, sister, five children, and wonderful wife. Josh would like to recognize his parents, grandmother, brother, two girls, and amazing wife. Thank you all for teaching us each day.

PUBLISHER'S ACKNOWLEDGMENTS

Corwin would like to thank the following individuals for their editorial insight and guidance:

Dr. James L. Drexler, dean of education
Covenant College
Lookout Mountain, GA

Dr. Gary Frye, homeless liaison/grant writer and executive director
Lubbock-Cooper ISD and Llano Estacado Rural Communities Foundation
Lubbock, TX

Dr. Douglas Gordon Hesbol, educational consultant and retired superintendent
Yorkville, IL

Jude A. Huntz, chancellor
Catholic Diocese of Kansas City
St. Joseph, MO

Dr. Gloria L. Johnston, retired superintendent of schools
Achievement Equity, Inc.
San Diego, CA

Dr. Bonnie Tryon, SAANYS representative
New York State Education Department's NCLB Committee of Practitioners
Cobleskill, NY

About the Authors

Gary W. Ritter is a professor of education policy and holder of the Endowed Chair in Education Policy in the Department of Education Reform at the University of Arkansas. He is also the director of the Office for Education Policy at the University of Arkansas, which to all interested constituents serves as a source of evidence and data on K–12 education in Arkansas. Currently, his primary area of interest is the development of alternative strategies for teacher compensation in public schools. His research interests also include program evaluation, school finance, standards-based and accountability-based school reform, and racial segregation in schools. Gary has been a faculty member at the University of Arkansas since earning a PhD in education policy in 2000 from the Graduate School of Education at the University of Pennsylvania. Gary currently teaches graduate courses in education policy, program evaluation, and research methods. His work has been published in various outlets, including *Phi Delta Kappan, Educational Leadership, Review of Educational Research, Education Finance & Policy, Educational Evaluation and Policy Analysis, Journal of Education Finance, American Review of Public Administration, International Journal of Testing, Georgetown Public Policy Review, Black Issues in Higher Education, Education Next,* and *Education Week.*

Gary's interest in studying and influencing educational policy was fueled by his first extended experience working with elementary students. In the 1990s, Gary spent several years in a variety of roles, including 4th grade teacher, physical education teacher, substitute teacher, track coach, and basketball coach, at an elementary school in inner-city Camden, New Jersey. Today, Gary puts most of his teaching and coaching energy into working with his five children in Fayetteville, Arkansas.

Joshua H. Barnett is an assistant professor of education policy and evaluation at Arizona State University. His primary research interest is improving the compensation structure in education, which includes how teachers and principals are evaluated and how resources are distributed. He has worked as a co-principal investigator on large-scale federal projects, including Teaching Quality Partnership and Teacher Incentive Fund grants. He has also worked across districts and states to help construct educator evaluation systems and professional development programs, and has developed numerous program evaluations at the school, district, and state level. His additional interests include teacher quality, fiscal issues around equity and adequacy, and program evaluation. Joshua joined ASU after serving as a Rotary Ambassadorial Scholar at Massey University in New Zealand and earning his PhD in public policy from the University of Arkansas. His work has been published in a variety of outlets, including *Review of Educational Research, Teachers College Record, Educational Leadership, Journal of Contemporary Issues in Education, New Zealand Education Review,* and *Issues in Teacher Education.*

Joshua's interest in reform issues resulted from his experience observing school disparities among different communities throughout his education. He worked toward reconciling school inequities as an intern in the Governor's office, a researcher at university, and a reading volunteer in a low-income school overseas. Throughout these experiences, the determining factor in schools—and in his personal life—was the vital role of great teachers.

Joshua spends his free time reading, playing sports, and supporting the Razorbacks. He is an active member of Christ's Church of the Valley, and he resides with his wife and girls in Phoenix, Arizona.

1

Introduction

*Merit Pay as Educational
Fad or Genuine Solution*

The last half of the 20th century witnessed the American educational system's transition from international leader to declining (or at least stagnant) star. For decades, Americans viewed the U.S. educational system as truly world class; however, this belief began waning sometime in the late 20th century, perhaps with the loss of the Space Race, the publication of *A Nation at Risk,* or the proliferation of policymakers continually arguing for improved education.

While the debate over the alleged "decline" of America's education system is ongoing, a great deal of evidence shows that national educational performance has remained somewhat stable over the past several decades. Regardless of how we as a nation began to lose faith in our perceived international ranking, continued international comparisons place students from the United States in the middle of the pack, and even well below their peers in many nations. Thus, the reality and the perception within and beyond America's borders is that America's schools are not among the "best and brightest."

As this recognition settles into the public psyche, policymakers and educational leaders continue to seek out and investigate comprehensive policy reforms to improve schools across the country. Changing the compensation structure of the educational workforce is one such reform. This book presents a straightforward conversation about the development, value, and process of creating a merit pay program.

WHAT IS MERIT PAY?

The concept of merit pay goes by many names and can take various forms. Sometimes referred to as *performance pay* or *incentive pay*, *merit pay* is a term describing a compensation formula based, at least in part, on performance, where different levels of pay are given to workers (teachers, administrators, or support staff) based on their differing levels of "effectiveness." Merit pay can be allocated to individuals through permanent additions to base salaries or through performance bonuses awarded at regular time intervals (e.g., annually). Most often, in the world of K–12 education, merit pay plans in existence or under consideration provide rewards through year-end performance bonuses.

Oftentimes, the merit pay conversation can venture into a broader discussion about differential pay for teachers. The question of differential pay is most often raised in the context of encouraging teachers to take on teaching roles that are hard to staff, such as those in less desirable environments or in academic areas characterized by teacher shortages (e.g., science or special education). While this type of market-based teacher compensation reform is interesting and does respond directly to clear problems inherent in the single-salary schedule, it will not be discussed here, as our focus rests squarely on merit pay.

For our purposes, we define merit pay programs as those that provide financial incentives to both reward exceptional classroom performance and to encourage a teacher to stay in the classroom. In their seminal systematic review of how merit pay programs have impacted student achievement, Podgursky and Springer (2007) established the following definition of merit pay:

> Merit-based pay rewards individual teachers, groups of teachers, or schools on any number of factors, including student performance, classroom observations, and teacher portfolios. Merit-based pay is a reward system that hinges on student outcomes attributed to a particular teacher or group of teachers rather than on "inputs" such as skills or knowledge. (p. 912)

The key component of this definition is that merit pay programs compensate teachers in a fundamentally different way than does the single-salary schedule. The single-salary system used by most districts and states provides teacher compensation bonuses for "inputs," such as years of experience or additional credentials. Merit-based compensation connects bonuses to performance or "outputs," such as gains in observation scores, portfolio assessments, and student achievement.

Why the Interest in Merit Pay?

Virtually every U.S. school official, education researcher, or interested citizen has a preferred remedy for low student achievement, particularly for disadvantaged learners. These remedies include instructional coaches, increased quality and quantity of professional development, smaller classes, longer school days, longer school years, single-gender classrooms, more time on task, and so on. But here's the problem: There's little conclusive evidence that any of these strategies consistently lead to improved student performance.

Evidence does reveal, however, that one element of the education mix consistently improves student performance: the presence of a high-quality teacher. Indeed, many researchers maintain that improving the quality of the nation's teaching force is the best policy intervention for raising student achievement (Goldhaber, 2002; Rivkin, Hanushek, & Kain, 2005). Grover J. Whitehurst, director of the Institute of Education Sciences, reported that a student who has effective teachers for 3 straight years is likely to score more than 50 percentile points higher on standardized tests than a student who has ineffective teachers (Whitehurst was drawing on research by Jordan, Mendro, & Weerasinghe, 1997; Rowan, 2002; Sanders & Rivers, 1996). The impact of having an effective teacher is enormous for a student if these gains are to be believed (and a growing body of research supports these claims). Advocates for merit pay are thus asking, Why are we focusing our attention on anything else? If teachers can have such a big impact, then perhaps the fundamental educational improvement strategy should be to ensure that every student has one of these "effective" teachers.

So how can policymakers increase the likelihood that students consistently have effective teachers? Many school reformers today are arguing that better systems of teacher compensation can be constructed to increase the number of effective teachers in classrooms across the nation.

Other strategies are being pursued to improve the effectiveness of classroom teachers; chief among these are innovative approaches to the initial preparation of teachers and to delivering effective professional development to teachers once they are in the profession. A variety of efforts are underway to improve these two avenues, and they have long since been part of the education reform conversation (see Darling-Hammond, 2006a, 2006b; Darling-Hammond & Sykes, 2003; Shulman, 1988; Wilson, Floden, & Ferrini-Mundy, 2001); however, the research on effective preparation and connecting it to effective practice has been tenuous (e.g., Cochran-Smith, Feiman-Nemser, McIntyre, & Demers, 2008; Good et al., 2006; Harris & Sass, 2007).

Notwithstanding the efforts to reform the preparation and development side, additional policies aimed at recruiting and retaining effective teachers are needed, and generally speaking, one of the consistent top reasons talented individuals choose not to enter or choose to leave the profession is compensation. And, in our view, the problems related to teacher compensation are far deeper than simply the level of pay. The next section discusses in detail the problems inherent in the current system.

WHAT'S WRONG WITH THE CURRENT SALARY SYSTEM?

About 95% of K–12 teachers in the United States work in a school or district with a salary schedule that provides pay based largely on years of experience and number of degrees attained (Podgursky & Springer, 2007). This "single-salary schedule" was developed explicitly to enhance equity for teachers in the 1920s. Prior to that time, teachers were paid differentially based on their position in the school. For example, elementary teachers were paid less than secondary teachers. The result was that women and minority teachers were generally paid less than white male teachers. Thus, the single-salary schedule was designed to pay the same salary to teachers with the same qualifications regardless of race, gender, or grade level taught. In this way, the justification for paying differential salary amounts was objective, measurable, and not subject to administrative whim.

Clearly, the development of the single-salary schedule was intended to foster fairness and equity in pay. Ironically, many critics of the uniform salary schedule claim that the way we currently pay teachers is inequitable in that it results in effective teachers being paid the same as ineffective teachers. Some reformers also argue that the current system is inequitable to poor students, as it limits the number of good teachers willing to work with economically disadvantaged students. But we'll talk more about this later. For now, let's go back to the problems with teacher compensation today.

In the single-salary system, compensation is seldom based on any evidence that a teacher is effective at enhancing student learning. This system assumes that teaching ability improves with more years of experience and higher degrees. However, many researchers argue that additional degrees do not translate into enhanced student performance and that the benefits of teacher experience plateau after several years (see, e.g., Goldhaber, 2002; Hanushek, 2003). If this finding is true (and it seems to be), the current teacher compensation structure is not likely to move the field forward in terms of boosting student achievement or ensuring that each child has an effective teacher. Teachers will get raises each year according to the salary schedule regardless of whether their work with students actually merits an increase in pay.

Indeed, there are many problems we might expect from the single-salary teacher pay structure. Or, better yet, there are various ways current teacher pay policies might be modified to improve the overall quality of the teacher workforce. We'll place them in three general categories, related to (1) the composition of individuals attracted to the teaching profession, (2) the motivation for teachers to improve within the current single-salary system, and (3) the rewards and retention possibilities for high-performing teachers.

First, the teaching profession as it is currently designed (and the single-salary structure in particular) allows very little room for upward growth; that is, regardless of what a teacher does, his or her salary will generally increase only with additional degrees or years of experience attained. This system is characterized by very high levels of job security in that teachers know with near certainty that they will retain their jobs year after year and what their salaries will be in a given year—and in the years that follow. This indicates that people drawn to the profession, overall, are those who desire stability and are not bothered by the limited possibilities for career advancement. Conversely, individuals who believe that they would do well in a differentiated system that rewards high performers may be discouraged from entering teaching as a lifelong career, as their high level of performance will never result in increased compensation (or recognition) in the current system. In other words, the current single-salary system may well dissuade potentially effective educators from entering the field and may keep in the field individuals who are comfortable with stability and consistency in their pay.

Second, the single-salary pay structure provides very little motivation (outside of the teacher's internal motivation) for working toward the strategic goals of the school or district. That is, whether a teacher chooses to focus on the standard district curricula or not (for example) is unlikely to affect that teacher's pay or job security. Thus, under the current single-salary structure, teacher pay cannot be used to motivate teachers to change their teaching strategies, to collaborate with their peers more, or to work harder. The current single-salary system simply does not allow school leaders to use compensation as a lever to motivate particular behaviors, efforts, or strategies from teachers.

Third, the single-salary pay structure provides school leaders very little leeway to use compensation to reward and retain particularly effective teachers. In fact, perverse incentives are built into the single-salary system that might encourage the best teachers to leave the classroom, because there are no monetary rewards tied to increased effort or effectiveness. As a result, the best teachers may choose to seek more "compensation" through a variety of channels that are not necessarily in the best interest of students in general. Consider these three common strategies through which effective teachers increase their overall "compensation":

1. Effective teachers may be rewarded with better working conditions; that is, they may seek out placements in high-income schools with student populations *viewed* as easier to educate.

2. Effective teachers may choose to leave the classroom altogether and enter school administration as a way to earn additional pay.

3. Effective teachers (who might prefer compensation in terms of dollars and cents rather than job security) may choose to leave the field of education altogether and pursue work in a field where they can receive greater financial rewards commensurate with their job performance.

In each of these three instances, the outcome is the opposite of what we want—*the single-salary structure incentivizes effective teachers to move farther away from the students who need them.* Merit pay advocates believe that teachers who prove themselves to be effective should be given opportunities to reap appropriate rewards while remaining in the field of education and in the classroom, where they can directly impact student learning. Furthermore, the most effective teachers should be encouraged to—rather than discouraged from—working with students in low-income areas with the greatest educational needs.

Perhaps most fundamentally, critics have complained that current practices related to teacher pay and employment include few, if any, consequences associated with good or bad performance. This is not only due to the single-salary schedule but also to the tenure rules employed in most school districts across the nation. That is, in other fields where employees do not benefit from the same level of job security afforded to teachers through the tenure process, poor job performance can lead to loss of employment. However, this is generally not the case in the field of teaching; indeed, even today, when dire budget circumstances in some states are leading to teacher layoffs, the layoff decisions are generally based on teacher seniority rather than on some measure of teacher performance (Goldhaber & Brewer, 1997; Goldhaber, DeArmond, Player, & Choi, 2008).

Thus, historically, the teaching profession is one with relatively few consequences—good or bad—related to performance. As a result, the calls for some type of merit pay are likely even louder in this field precisely because these merit bonuses represent the only mechanism to encourage better or different job performance!

HOW MIGHT MERIT PAY HELP?

Merit pay programs are intended to positively impact the teaching corps in two ways—through motivational impacts and compositional impacts. First, proponents contend that the possibility of earning financial rewards based on increased student achievement will motivate current teachers to focus their efforts on student achievement in the measured subjects through innovation and additional effort.

Here we must be clear—the motivation aspect of merit pay is more complicated than imagining that teachers will simply work harder if that additional work might result in additional pay. Surely, this would be the case for some, but many others are likely working at their maximum level of effort already. However, teachers may well work very hard in areas that are not consistent with the school's mission, or particular curricular standards. A merit pay plan that rewards the extent to which students can master the school's "standards" will most certainly encourage teachers to focus on those curricular guidelines. Indeed, there are likely many teachers who are excellent at engaging students and delivering compelling lessons that are not in line with the district or state's curricula. While these lessons may be engaging for the students and particularly interesting to the teacher, they may not build foundational skills the students will need in the years that follow. In the absence of any external pressures, the teacher may feel comfortable focusing on whatever content he or she deems important, rather than on the content required by the state or district curricular guidelines.

Perhaps most important, this issue arises in the form of those teachers who simply believe their course materials are "good enough" and have been for years. This issue affects those teachers who have not and do not plan to adjust to the changing times or changing curriculum. In many schools, these teachers are tenured and are not subject to dismissal and can choose to ignore curricular changes; however, merit pay provides one method to address such teachers directly.

As famed economist Ed Lazear (2003) noted,

> Teachers may be very hard-working in general, but individual teachers may believe that some things are more important than others in the curriculum. A teacher with idiosyncratic views might provide the wrong kind of education to his or her students. Tying compensation to the appropriate metric provides incentives to move in the direction that has been agreed on. (p. 182)

Thus, merit pay advocates hope that school leaders may use pay to motivate some teachers to work harder but also to encourage some otherwise excellent teachers to work differently by ensuring that they give consideration to the agreed-on curricular standards when developing their lessons.

Second, proponents of this strategy hypothesize that merit pay programs could have a positive influence on the composition of the teacher workforce in two ways: (1) increasing the applicant pool and (2) encouraging the best teachers to stay in the classroom. A larger pool of applicants—and perhaps even a more talented pool of candidates—may be drawn into the profession if they believed their talent will be rewarded. As we suggested earlier, teachers who enter the profession today can expect very little room for upward growth but very high levels of job security. This system may well discourage young people from considering teaching as a career option if these young people are confident that they would flourish in a differentiated system that rewards high performers. If, on the other hand, the profession were to reward effectiveness through financial incentives, these self-assured individuals might be more likely to enter the profession and might well turn out to be very effective in the classroom.

Moreover, if a merit pay program operated well, it would also foster a more effective teaching corps over time. That is, under a merit-based scheme, the most effective teachers would consistently earn large bonuses, their less effective peers would earn lesser rewards, and ineffective teachers would receive very little in the way of performance bonuses. We would expect a sort of "natural selection" whereby the more effective teachers, encouraged by their annual recognition and rewards, would continue to teach. On the other hand, teachers who continually experienced negative feedback through the annual evaluation and merit pay system would find the job of teaching less rewarding and would begin to seek out other career options or would work to improve their skills. Over time, this process could lead to a systematic change of the teacher workforce in which the most effective teachers stay in the field and serve as role models while those who are not suited to the profession choose not to stay.

In the abstract, this type of system seems optimal for both students and teachers. Under this plan, excellent teachers would not feel the need to leave the profession to seek recognition elsewhere, and those who struggle would be encouraged to find a job that would be a better fit for them. And children would be more likely to be sitting in classrooms with effective teachers who feel appropriately recognized and rewarded. This seems like a no-brainer, right? So why aren't all schools and districts using merit pay rather than the current outdated system? Well, it's complicated.

Why Is Merit Pay So Complicated?

When a district uses a merit pay plan, it typically creates a system for evaluating teacher performance and examines the teachers in the district regularly to see how they are performing. A teacher who routinely performs above the standard may be awarded a monetary bonus for his or her work, while other teachers are kept at the regular pay standard. Of course, the sticking point here is the method for evaluating teacher performance. While some critics balk at the general idea of any type of merit pay, others may be in favor of the concept of merit pay but wary of the teacher evaluation tools that might be employed. In developing a potentially effective plan, school leaders must ask many questions and make several important decisions regarding the way the educators in the school are to be evaluated.

We will dig into these questions in much more detail throughout the remaining chapters, where we will discuss all the decisions that must be made in developing a thoughtful plan (and we will weigh in with our views on how best to make these decisions); however, three key issues are worth noting briefly here.

Key Issue 1: Evaluation Tools

Most merit pay advocates insist that teacher "merit" be based, at least in part, on the measured achievement of the students in the teacher's class-·room. Not surprisingly, the idea of holding teachers accountable for their students' standardized test score gains is a source of great debate and discord (see Amrein-Beardsley, 2012; Harris, 2011). Nevertheless, most merit pay plans do and will include standardized measures of student achievement. *Thus, school leaders must make decisions regarding which tests are to be used, which students are to be counted for which teachers, and how test score gains are to be calculated.*

Of course, an evaluation of merit could also include numerous other, non-test-score components. Examples of these include teacher experience, credentials, classroom observations, and principal ratings, as well as many less standard measures based on other student outcomes and parent and student opinions. *As a result, school leaders must decide to what extent non-test-score measures are incorporated into the merit evaluation system.*

Key Issue 2: Group or Individual Awards

Another point of contention in the merit pay debate revolves around the group to be rewarded. That is, should a merit pay plan assign merit ratings to groups of teachers or to individual teachers? Some merit pay plans today are school based; that is, the school receives some sort of rating for its overall performance over a given time period. Then, all the teachers in that school receive a bonus based on the "merit" of the school as a whole. Other plans rate individual teachers based on their classroom performance and allocate different reward levels to different teachers. *So school leaders must also decide whether to rate teachers based only on the students in their particular classes or on the outcomes for a wider group of students that may well have been influenced by each particular teacher.*

Key Issue 3: Defining Program Participants and Award Levels

There is also the question of which school employees are eligible for the merit pay program. In schools or districts with the most limited programs, only those teachers who teach "core" subjects with related standardized assessments can participate. In other plans, non-core teachers and school support staff are eligible for awards, although the award levels and rating systems might be different. Finally, some merit pay plans include awards for school administrators based on overall performance of the school or district. *Therefore, school leaders must also decide which types of educators and school employees to include in the bonus pool and what levels of rewards to offer to each type of employee.*

In general, the takeaway from this section is that there is no single merit pay "plan"; instead, there are numerous ways school leaders could implement a merit pay scheme for their educators. Thus, clearly, one could imagine a merit pay scheme designed poorly or designed well. Indeed, this is the primary reason a book such as this one can serve as a useful guide to program developers as they make important decisions regarding program design details. Throughout this book, we will walk through each of the most important issues school leaders must address as they develop and implement a thoughtful plan to incorporate a performance component into their current teacher compensation schemes. We begin by examining the landscape of policies ushering in the new wave of compensation reforms and why these reforms are occurring now.

2

Why Is Merit Pay Gaining Momentum?

A Brief History

Within the U.S. education system, efforts to reform teacher compensation have existed at least since the 1920s (Murnane & Cohen, 1986). These efforts reach even further back abroad, where performance-pay programs developed, at least in part, from the Newcastle Commission's recommendation that "distinct inducements" be awarded to teachers "so that they would bring up their individual scholars . . . to a certain mark" ("The Royal Commission," 1861, p. 274). Recognizing that this strategy has ebbed and flowed over a century and a half, many educators and practitioners may be wondering why this policy is once again emerging. In Chapter 3, we discuss the evidence base and research surrounding merit pay; however, in this chapter, we address the momentum behind merit pay across local, state, and national contexts and provide a summary of where it is occurring. The value of this chapter is that research and evidence generally take months or even years to emerge once a program is in place, so we want to provide a discussion of how merit pay is developing with anticipation that more evidence will continue to emerge in the years ahead.

The debate over merit pay is generally straightforward and has created two rather entrenched camps. Supporters of performance pay contend that replacing the single-salary schedules with financial incentives based at least partially on results will motivate teachers to improve instruction and will recruit better teachers to the field. Opponents argue that such a change will diminish teachers' intrinsic motivation and lead to perverse incentives. Researchers have significantly influenced these policy debates (Wilson, Floden, & Ferrini-Mundy, 2001), and many of these discussions are grounded in economic assumptions about labor markets, employee behavior, and incentives (Murnane & Cohen, 1986).

Over the past quarter century, the spirit of reforming the single-salary schedule has resulted in several large-scale programs, including performance-based pay, career ladders (usually based on responsibilities), and differential pay (usually based on subject or geographic area). The intent behind these various programs, however, generally waned quickly and resulted in poorly implemented programs that existed for short periods of time (Glazerman, 2004). As supporters of compensation reform have examined why such programs fared so poorly, several key factors have emerged. Specifically, implementation challenges have historically developed from a lack of objective, reliable measures of teacher performance, uncertainty from stakeholders about how to develop different pay scales for teachers, and the cost of sustaining such programs (Belfield & Heywood, 2007; Glazerman, 2004; Hanushek, 2007; Hassel & Hassel, 2007; Heck, 2009; Murnane & Cohen, 1986; Podgursky, 2002; Silman & Glazerman, 2009).

Over the past decade, researchers have made grand strides in addressing these concerns across two dimensions. First, the 2002 passage of the No Child Left Behind Act (NCLB) dramatically improved the frequency and coverage of standardized student assessments by requiring that all students in Grades 3 through 8 be tested using a standard-based metric. An outgrowth of this requirement was the development of more sophisticated data-tracking systems (Glazerman et al., 2010). As a natural by-product of having year-to-year data, researchers began considering how to make use of these data, where students who are perpetual high or low performers can be tracked for "growth" rather than performance. The opportunity to track students brought forth the ability to calculate value-added achievement scores, which substantively addressed the previous concern about the lack of an objective, reliable measure of teacher performance.

Second, NCLB's accountability efforts brought forth much more sophisticated data-tracking advancements in technology. States now needed to warehouse data and redistribute it back to the schools in a much more efficient and proactive manner. While the real value of this element for practitioners is still being debated, the argument that NCLB encouraged state departments of education to collect, warehouse, examine, and provide more data to educators is difficult to dispute.

With voluminous data emerging, compensation reformers reappeared to begin examining how these data could be used to address prior concerns over unreliable and unstable measures. Consistent with this emergence, a decade since NCLB, the term *value-added* is now familiar to virtually every teacher, principal, and person in the education community. Strides continue to be made regarding the reliability and validity of value-added measures (see Amrein-Beardsley, 2012, and Harris, 2011); however, these measures need improving. As the technology and accountability developments paved the way to address some prior reservations regarding performance pay, local, state, and national initiatives have brought the debate over compensation to the forefront of the education reform agenda.

In 2007, the U.S. Department of Education awarded 34 grantees through the Teacher Incentive Fund (TIF). State and local initiatives included Minnesota's Q-Comp program ($86 million), Nevada's teacher bonus programs ($65 million), New York City's Partnership for Teaching Excellence ($15 million granted by the Carrol and Milton Petrie Foundation), and a multisite investment of $370 million by the Bill & Melinda Gates Foundation to reform teacher compensation in Pittsburgh, Pennsylvania; Memphis, Tennessee; Hillsborough County, Florida; and a consortium of charter schools in California (Glazerman et al., 2011).

Additionally, the 2009 American Recovery and Reinvestment Act allocated about $100 billion to the Department of Education in support of programs to improve public education. Once again, TIF was designated as a piece of the puzzle and distributed nearly $450 million for performance-based teacher and principal compensation systems.

As states, districts, and individual schools have examined how to apply for and make use of these resources, a few larger scale organizations have emerged as part of the discussion. For example, several TIF applicants employ the Teacher Advancement Program (TAP), a comprehensive teacher-pay reform model that provides performance-based pay, multiple career paths for educators, ongoing applied professional development, and instructionally focused accountability. The TAP model includes evaluations based on student achievement and classroom-observation scores, and offers merit payments. TAP is currently in schools across the nation, affecting about 20,000 teachers and 200,000 students (http://tapsystem.org).

Beyond the national initiatives, several states have developed their own plans to adjust what they view as an outdated compensation structure. One of the leading states on this front is Texas, which began creating payout differences in the 1980s (Springer, Lewis, Podgursky, Ehlert, Gronberg et al., 2009; Springer, Lewis, Podgursky, Ehlert, Taylor et al., 2009). Texas has implemented several large-scale pay-for-performance incentive programs with a combination of state and federal funding. These programs include the

Governor's Educator Excellence Grant (GEEG), Texas Educator Excellence Grant (TEEG), and District Awards for Teacher Excellence (DATE). Both GEEG and TEEG provided grants to implement pay-for-performance bonuses for teachers at schools with high or improved student achievement and serving a high percentage of economically disadvantaged students. The culmination of these programs was DATE, which resulted in about $900 million in total funding over the 4-year lifespan of the policy. More than 200 districts participated in creating their own "locally grown" performance-pay programs.

Following the advancement in accountability and technology during the previous decade and associated with NCLB, other states and local agencies have created smaller scale programs that are receiving much recognition—for example, Guilford, North Carolina; Nashville, Tennessee; and New York City. The TIF-funded program in North Carolina's Guilford County Schools is a comprehensive recruitment and retention program that includes performance bonuses ranging from $2,500 to $5,000, as well as recruitment bonuses, professional development, performance accountability, and structural support.

The Project on Incentives in Teaching program in Nashville, Tennessee, offered substantial performance bonuses (ranging from $5,000 to $15,000) to middle school math teachers whose students achieved significant gains on standardized tests, and the highest performing teachers were eligible to receive bonuses substantially larger than that of the average teacher. Math teachers were given the opportunity to participate in a 3-year experiment in which participants were randomly assigned either to be eligible for the pay-for-performance bonuses or to the control condition, which was the usual salary schedule. The experiment included 296 teachers at the beginning of the first year, but there was substantial attrition from the sample and only 148 teachers participated by the third year (Springer, Ballou et al., 2010).

The Schoolwide Performance Bonus Program in New York City was implemented in about 200 K–12 public schools in 2007–2008 and 2008–2009 (Fryer, 2011; Goodman & Turner, 2010; Marsh et al., 2011). Schools that met student-achievement performance targets could earn up to $3,000 per full-time union member at the school. In each school, a school-level compensation committee decided how bonuses would be distributed and, in most cases, all teachers received the same bonus when their school achieved the student performance target.

These programs and others highlight an interest in movement away from the single-salary system and toward a revised compensation structure. The next chapter examines these programs with an eye toward their impact on student achievement and teacher quality. While not all of these studies have produced results to this point, they, again, show that local, state, and federal education agencies are continuing to advance the conversation toward reforming educator compensation.

3

What Can a Merit Plan Do for Your Teachers and Students?

Teachers matter. So instead of bashing them, or defending the status quo, let's offer schools a deal. Give them the resources to keep good teachers on the job, and reward the best ones. And in return, grant schools flexibility: to teach with creativity and passion; to stop teaching to the test; and to replace teachers who just aren't helping kids learn. That's a bargain worth making.

—President Barack Obama, 2012 State of the Union Address

President Obama noted that we should "give them [schools] the resources to keep good teachers on the job, and reward the best ones." The question to policymakers and educators alike is, how can this be accomplished? This chapter explores the current knowledge base around merit pay systems. The value of this chapter is that it presents how these programs have performed in totality, even though each program discussed varies in design and implementation. This chapter should be examined in combination with Chapter 2, which presents the movement toward merit pay, as this chapter explains the current status of that movement via impact to teachers and students.

How much money should America's public school teachers earn? Any talk of "teacher salaries" generally elicits a spirited response from both practitioners and policymakers, with teachers generally arguing that they are underpaid and policymakers unsure of how to improve the system aside from providing flat increases for all teachers. Many observers maintain that the flaw in teacher salaries is not the overall level of pay but, instead, the structure of the payment schedule. For nearly five decades, the single-salary schedule, whereby teachers are paid on the basis of tenure and degrees earned, has been in place across the nation (Odden, 2000). In fact, national survey data indicate that about 95% of the 15,000 public school districts use the single-salary pay system (Podgursky, 2007). This means that more than 3 million public school teachers are paid on variables—experience and education level—that are weakly related to the academic performance of students (Hanushek, 2003).

Despite the single-salary schedule's popularity and longevity, a growing number of observers are arguing that it has produced problems in America's schools, including problems with getting high-quality teachers into the classroom, retaining them in the profession, and holding them accountable for student achievement (Goldhaber, 2002; Plucker, Zapf, & McNabb, 2005). Due to these perceived problems, some states and districts (e.g., Charlotte-Mecklenburg, Cincinnati, Denver, Douglas County, Nevada, Los Angeles, Texas, and Washoe County) and the federal government via the Teacher Incentive Fund are moving incrementally away from the single-salary schedule in hopes of recruiting and retaining more qualified teachers who can improve student performance (Kelley, 1998, 2000; Odden & Kelley, 1997).

However, each district that ventures out in this area seems to be operating within a vacuum, trying to develop new merit-based systems with little knowledge of the effectiveness or characteristics of other performance pay systems. Candidly put, those pushing for and those interested in exploring merit pay programs need more information to make informed decisions for revising the teacher compensation system.

This chapter in particular—and this book overall—responds explicitly to the gap in information by reviewing and describing the extant literature. Through a systematic review of the literature, we provide an overview of the most important characteristics of several recently-developed teacher pay systems in which financial incentives for teachers are linked to student performance. Moreover, we believe that policymakers will find this easy-to-digest summary of information valuable. The studies described below have different methodological (type of analysis used to determine the impact) and theoretical (i.e., individual or group reward) issues; however, we are presenting a culmination of the available evidence to help support the conclusions we draw in future chapters, where we sift through these and additional studies to provide concrete examples of the types of programs we believe are most effective.

This chapter is separated into four sections. First, we briefly discuss why so few rigorous evaluations exist. Second, we review the evidence on the impact of merit pay on teachers. Third, we consider the evidence on the impact of merit pay on student achievement. Fourth, this chapter closes with conclusions based on the evidence of merit pay programs.

EVIDENCE ON MERIT PAY

According to McCarty (1986), merit pay seems to take hold of the education world every 20 years or so; despite these regular recurrences, we have little if any good evidence on what happens when such programs are implemented. Murnane and Cohen (1986) noted that merit pay programs typically do not persist for extended periods of time due to the considerable financial costs associated with providing bonuses to teachers and school employees, and because merit pay programs typically face a great deal of opposition from teacher groups who question the fairness of compensating personnel based on allegedly dubious measures of teacher effectiveness. Ballou (2001) also cited budgetary constraints as a primary reason for the short shelf life of these programs. Administrators in unionized school systems likely face considerable difficulty maintaining these programs due to the opposition from teachers and have little incentive to even undertake these often unpopular reform efforts in the first place.

As discussed in Chapter 2, what is different in today's American educational culture is the full swing toward accountability and the ability to measure, track, and interpret the performance of students and teachers. Additionally, the economic downturn of the first decade of the 21st century continues to force a critical lens over all programs operating in schools—where those that are not effectively leading to improvement are traded for those with more promise. As noted in the section below, the evidence from merit pay evaluations indicates that they can be a powerful and positive policy tool to improve school climates and student performance.

Studies on Teacher Attitudes

While the research community does not know much about the impact of merit pay plans on teacher attitudes, we do have information from eight programs operating in various schools across the United States (for more information about programs operating internationally, see Barnett & Openshaw, 2011, and Harvey-Beavis, 2003). Each of these plans and the corresponding influence on teacher attitudes is described below.

Tennessee Master Teacher Plan

In 1988, Horace Johns evaluated the Tennessee Master Teacher Plan (see Handler & Carlson, 1984, for a full program description). The program was designed to improve teacher motivation and reduce teacher alienation, and thus increase the recruitment and retention of high-quality teachers. The program, proposed by then-Governor Lamar Alexander, held that teachers would progress through four stages from apprentice teacher to master teacher, each with a corresponding salary bonus based on performance and classroom observations.

For the evaluation, Johns (1988) randomly selected 1,500 teachers from the 28,000 K–12 classroom teachers in Tennessee. Of those 1,500 teachers, 927 (61.8%) returned the survey, which asked a series of questions in an effort to understand three issues. First, how do the teachers of Tennessee perceive the plan? Second, do teachers feel more or less motivated by the plan? Third, do teachers feel more or less alienated by the plan? Of survey participants, 91% reported that the plan was not a significant factor in making them want to keep teaching, 92% reported that the plan did not increase morale for teachers, 91% reported that the plan did not increase their enthusiasm for teaching, and 89% stated that other methods would be better for recruiting and retaining high-quality teachers. Overall, the findings for this evaluation are negative.

Utah Career Ladder Program

In 1993, Horan and Lambert (1994) conducted an evaluation of the Utah Career Ladder Program. The Career Ladder Program was intended to attract and retain "good" teachers and improve the quality of schools in Utah. The program consisted of five components, including performance bonuses, new-teacher incentives, job enlargement, extended contract days, and staff development. Each district was able to determine the minimum qualifications for the performance bonuses. In total, the state paid out about $4.5 million to 40 school districts for the bonuses. For this evaluation, 836 surveys were mailed to teachers and principals in all 40 districts where the Career Ladder Program was operating. Additionally, 13 focus-group interviews were conducted with 206 teachers and seven principals, and 40 telephone interviews were conducted.

Ninety percent of the teachers and principals believed that the extended days and staff development improved their working environment and enhanced the teaching profession. Teachers and principals provided mixed reviews of the performance-bonus and ladder levels, indicating that these were important components, but less important than other aspects of the program. With regard to student achievement, 90% of the respondents indicated that the program improved the educational programs within the schools, and more than 60% of principals responded that the program had a positive effect on student achievement.

The evaluation also highlighted some problem areas. Specifically, the evaluation indicated that the performance bonus component may be administered unfairly and that the evaluation process for receiving such bonuses was not completely understood. Some teachers also acknowledged that the program increased competition within the schools, but this competition was seen as positive by some and negative by others. Overall, the findings for this evaluation are mixed due to both positive and negative results.

Denver Merit Pay Program

The Community Training and Assistance Center (2004) evaluated the impact of a merit pay program that operated in schools in Denver, Colorado, in which teachers could earn a fixed amount as a bonus for achieving teacher-created objectives by the end of the school year. The bonuses were $750 for one objective or $1,500 for two objectives (e.g., 90% of students performing at the proficient level in reading). The researchers found that teachers in Denver schools using this merit pay program reported higher levels of access to student testing data, an increased focus on student achievement, and improved collegiality among teachers. However, these teachers also reported that the merit pay program did not affect their teaching style in a significant way.

Arkansas Merit Pay Program

Barnett, Ritter, Winters, and Greene (2007) evaluated the Achievement Challenge Pilot Project (ACPP) operating within the Little Rock School District. This program provided an opportunity to conduct a rigorous evaluation to uncover the effects of a merit pay program on student achievement (discussed later under the student subsection), as well as on the behaviors and attitudes of teachers with regard to innovation, working harder, satisfaction, competition, environment, and openness to challenges. The question was whether the arguments of those who support or those who oppose merit pay would be revealed in this program. The ACPP provided bonuses to teachers based solely on student performance, where higher bonuses were attached to higher achievement growth from year to year as measured by the state's standardized test. The data for teachers were collected via surveys of the teachers' attitudes. Based on the comparison of teachers in the ACPP schools with teachers not in the ACPP schools, the following findings emerged:

- Teachers in the merit pay program reported that they were no more innovative than comparison teachers.

- Teachers in the merit pay program reported that they were no more likely to work harder than were comparison teachers.
- Teachers in the merit pay program reported that they were more satisfied with their salaries than were comparison teachers.
- Teachers in the merit pay program reported no more counterproductive competition than did comparison teachers.
- Teachers in the merit pay program reported that their work environment became more positive than that of comparison teachers.
- Teachers in the merit pay program were less likely than comparison teachers to agree that low-performing students were a burden in the classroom.
- Teachers in the merit pay program were more likely than comparison teachers to report that the academic performance of their students had improved over the past year.

Three Texas Merit Pay Programs

More recently, the National Center for Performance Incentives conducted evaluations on three merit pay programs operating in the state of Texas: the Texas Educator Excellence Grant program (Springer, Lewis, Podgursky, Ehlert, Gronberg et al., 2009); the Governor's Educator Excellence Grant program (Springer, Lewis, Podgursky, Ehlert, Taylor et al., 2009); and the District Awards for Teacher Excellence program (DATE; Springer, Lewis et al., 2010). These programs, which affected more than 250 schools and 80,000 school personnel, allowed the school leaders to determine how best to allocate a fixed amount of funds. The average bonus across the three programs was about $2,000 (ranging from roughly $1,350 to $3,350) per teacher.

According to the evaluations, these programs did not adversely affect collaboration or collegiality in the schools; rather, teachers reported that the programs positively affected the school climate. The evaluations also found that the turnover rate in the schools using the merit pay programs was significantly less than in the nonprogram schools. However, even with these findings, the teachers also reported that their teaching styles did not change as a result of the programs.

Survey of Teachers Nationwide

The final rigorously designed evaluation of the impact of merit pay programs on teachers did find adverse effects. However, this evaluation, conducted by Belfield and Heywood (2007), examined teacher attitudes and perceptions toward merit pay as reported from the nationally administered Schools and Staffing Survey. The researchers found that teachers participating in merit pay programs reported being no more satisfied with their careers than teachers in non-merit-pay schools/districts. However, the researchers did find that teachers in merit pay schools reported being more dissatisfied with their salaries than did their non-merit-pay peers. While this finding seems counterintuitive, the researchers contended that "merit pay may put income at risk, involve negative comparisons, and generate peer pressure or extra effort" (p. 250).

Even though this study concluded that teachers in merit pay programs report lower rates of salary satisfaction, there are several reasons to ask questions about this study. Namely, the responses were from 60,000 teachers working in a variety of programs, in a variety of schools, with a variety of bonus amounts, and affected by a variety of other factors. However, this study provides a good reminder that, as we discussed previously, the devil is in the details! The potential of any merit pay program depends a great deal on how the program is developed, implemented, and discussed with teachers.

Based on the findings from these eight studies, we conclude that— generally speaking—merit pay programs have a positive impact on the teaching morale and school climate. Specifically, in the strongest studies, teachers report an increased focus on student achievement, increased access to student data, lower teacher turnover, and a positive school environment. Perhaps the most important elements to know—based on the evidence from these evaluations—is that merit pay programs did not lead to some of the often-cited concerns regarding these programs. Specifically, the merit pay programs did not lead to increased levels of negative competition and alienation. This overall conclusion is important to consider within the context that programs continue to evolve as new data continue to emerge and inform program developers. As we continue to reiterate, programs are often tailored to the individual school, but a thorough examination of the literature indicates that successful programs do contain certain key elements (a topic we return to in the examples discussed in Chapter 6).

The attitudes and behaviors of the teachers are important to note; however, the impact on student performance is also of the utmost concern for those considering the development and implementation of a merit pay program. The next section examines what the literature provides with regard to impact of such programs on student achievement.

Studies on Student Achievement

South Carolina Teacher Incentive Programs

Cohn and Teel (1991) evaluated the relationship between student achievement and teacher participation in various incentive programs operating across South Carolina during the 1988–1989 school year. The South Carolina Teacher

Incentive Program awarded annual bonuses of $2,000 to $3,000 to teachers based on two criteria: (1) individual bonus plan that rewarded teachers based on attendance, performance evaluation, self-improvement, and student achievement and (2) collective awards to staff members in schools with high levels of student achievement. A stratified random sample of schools was selected and matched to a comparison group of nonparticipating schools. Reading and/or math teachers in Grades 1 through 6 were selected to participate in the study. Results showed that students in incentive-program schools earned higher gain scores in reading and math compared with students in nonparticipating schools.

Dallas Accountability and Incentive Program

Ladd (1999) evaluated the effect of the Dallas Accountability and Incentive Program. During the first 3 years of the program, financial bonuses were provided for all members of the school, where principals and teachers received bonuses of $1,000, and other staff members, including janitors and secretaries, received bonuses of $500. Each high-performing school was also awarded $2,000. One of the biggest complaints about the program was that it ranked schools rather than having schools compete against predetermined standards. Ladd also noted that "school officials could manipulate the system by keeping some children from being tested or by outright cheating" (p. 3).

Program effectiveness was determined by three measures: the pass rates on the reading and mathematics portions of the Texas Assessment of Academic Skills (TAAS) for students in seventh grade, the student dropout rates in high school, and the turnover rate of principals. Schools and students in five other large Texas cities were used as comparison groups.

Ladd (1999) noted mixed findings in her study, including consistent and positive large findings for Hispanic and white students but smaller findings for black students on the TAAS exam. The study also noted a decrease in the Dallas dropout rate and higher turnover among principals relative to comparison cities. Ladd posited that the higher turnover among principals was a positive finding since these principals were removed from the district rather than being transferred around the district, which showed that the administration was serious about removing ineffective leadership.

Community High School Pilot Program, Michigan

In 2002, Eberts, Hollenbeck, and Stone evaluated one program that operated in one high school in Michigan. The Community High School pilot program included a performance-based payout scheme for teachers; however, this institution is an alternative high school with about 500 students. Teachers in the Community High School received a 12.5% bonus to their base salary if more than 80% of their students remained enrolled in the school at the end of the year. Another alternative high school was selected as a comparison. The evaluation found that dropout rates decreased. However, Eberts et al. acknowledged that the pass rates and schoolwide grade point average in the program school decreased as a result of more students remaining in the school, which makes sense since low-achieving students who would have previously dropped out remained in school. One of the key limitations discussed in this study is that the program was limited to a single school (pilot program); as such, the conclusions are difficult to generalize.

Tennessee Career Ladder Plan

Dee and Keys (2004, 2005) evaluated the Tennessee Career Ladder Plan by asking whether teachers choosing to participate in the plan fostered greater increases in student achievement than did their nonparticipating peers. The unique facet of this study is that the students were randomly assigned to teachers, which was a fortuitous outcome of the Student/Teacher Achievement Ratio project. The Tennessee Career Ladder Plan awarded merit pay supplements to teachers for earning favorable evaluations and climbing up the career ladder. Dee and Keys found that Career Ladder participants were more effective than their peers. Students assigned to a teacher who was certified on the career ladder experienced statistically significant gains in both math and reading.

Arizona Career Ladder Program

Dowling, Murphy, and Wang (2007) compared the student achievement results of career-ladder districts and non-career-ladder districts across the state of Arizona. Consistent with the theory of performance pay programs, the Arizona Career Ladder Program was "intended to increase student achievement by attracting and retaining talented teachers" (p. 3). According to the report, the Career Ladder Program included about 30% of all students and 40% of all teachers in the state. The evaluation of the program compared the career-ladder and non-career-ladder districts on student achievement in math, reading, and writing using the Arizona Instrument to Measure Standards (AIMS) for 2004–2005 and 2005–2006, and attendance data for 2004–2005 and 2005–2006. The comparisons of schools were matched on three characteristics: size of community, school enrollment, and socioeconomic status as measured by free/reduced-priced lunch percentage.

Using a series of regression models controlling for size, location, and socioeconomic status, Dowling et al. (2007) found that students in the career-ladder schools had higher overall AIMS passing rates (combined subjects). Further, the authors found that students in the career-ladder schools had higher math, reading, and writing scores, indicating a positive relationship between each subject area and participation in the career-ladder program. No differences were found with regard to attendance rates in the study.

National Education Longitudinal Survey and Schools and Staffing Survey

Figlio and Kenny (2006) used data from the National Education Longitudinal Survey and the Schools and Staffing Survey. Within these national datasets, Figlio and Kenny created an indicator for merit pay schemes in schools. Unlike the previously discussed studies, which focused on distinct schools that either had a program or did not, the researchers were able to determine a "dosage," or degree, of merit pay used in hundreds of schools across the country and examine subsequent effects. The researchers noted that

> students learn more in schools in which individual teachers are given financial incentives to do a better job, though [they] cannot discern whether this relationship is due to incentives themselves or to better schools also choosing to implement merit pay programs. (pp. 17–18)

Arkansas Merit Pay Program

Winters, Ritter, Barnett, and Greene (2008) evaluated the impact of a merit pay program operating across three elementary schools in Little Rock, Arkansas (see also Winters, Ritter, Greene, & Marsh, 2009). In this program, all school personnel (i.e., custodians, staff, teachers, principals) could earn a year-end bonus if student achievement improved in the school. Under this program, teachers could earn a bonus that ranged from $0 to $12,000. The researchers measured the level of student achievement growth in math, reading, and language for students in the fourth and fifth grade in schools with merit pay, compared with students in demographically similar schools. The researchers found that students in merit pay schools had test score gains, expressed in Normal Curve Equivalent points, that were 3.6 to 4.6 points greater than the gains observed for students in demographically similar comparison schools.

California Merit Pay Program

In 2009, Bacolod, DiNardo, and Jacobson evaluated the impact of a merit pay program that operated from 2000 to 2002 in California. The average amount of the bonuses for teachers was about $1,900 dollars, and all employees in the school were eligible for the bonus amount. The researchers noted that the program was associated with "little measurable improvements in . . . [student] achievement" (p. 5). However, the researchers also note that the program experienced several challenges, including changing the eligibility requirements across the 2 years of implementation and not rewarding teachers based on their individual contributions.

Texas DATE Program

In the evaluation of the impact of the DATE program in Texas, Springer, Lewis et al. (2010) concluded that students in DATE schools made larger gains on the Texas state assessment compared with students in non-DATE schools. In this program, schools or districts were allowed to design merit pay programs that rewarded teachers based primarily on measures of student achievement. About 50% of teachers in the 203 DATE schools earned a bonus, with average bonuses ranging from $1,361 for those teachers under a districtwide plan to $3,344 for teachers under a schoolwide plan.

Nashville Project on Incentives in Teaching

The Project on Incentives in Teaching (POINT) program operated for a 3-year period in the Nashville School District. Middle school math teachers in the POINT program could earn bonuses of $5,000, $10,000, or $15,000 for demonstrating substantial impact on growth levels for students in their classrooms (e.g., the maximum bonus of $15,000 could be earned if a teacher's students performed in the 95th percentile in math). The evaluation of this program (Springer, Ballou et al., 2010) found a significant difference in the performance of fifth-grade students in merit-pay-eligible and non-merit-pay-eligible classrooms. The study, however, did not find this difference in Grades 6 through 8. A key finding from this study is the distinction between the significant finding for grade levels where the students remained in a single classroom (fifth grade) compared with grade levels where students moved between classrooms (sixth grade through eighth grade).

New York City Merit Pay Program

Similar to the examination of the evidence with regard to teacher attitudes, we located a single study where a merit pay program was associated with negative findings on student performance. Fryer's (2011) investigation of a citywide, merit pay program implemented in New York City showed lower achievement for the students in merit pay program schools. In the New York merit pay program, schools were randomly assigned to participate. If the students in a participating school achieved at a predetermined performance level, then the school received a lump sum equal to $3,000 per school employee to be distributed at the discretion of a committee of teachers and school personnel (i.e., evenly among all employees or differentially among various employees).

Fryer (2011) noted that this program resulted in no instances of positive increases in student achievement, and at the middle school level, participating schools actually experienced lower student achievement than did the comparison schools. The New York City program was also evaluated previously by Springer and Winters (2009). In their examination, they found the program had no impact on student achievement.

Merit Pay in Denver Public Schools

An evaluation of the merit pay in Denver Public Schools (Community Training and Assistance Center, 2004; described previously) showed mixed findings for student achievement. For middle and high school students, the program corresponded to improvement in three of the six achievement measures; however, for elementary school students, the program corresponded to improvement in only one of the six achievement measures.

National Institute for Excellence in Teaching's Teacher Advancement Program

Springer, Ballou, and Peng (2008) conducted an evaluation of the National Institute for Excellence in Teaching's Teacher Advancement Program (TAP), operating across two unidentified states. For the TAP merit pay calculations, 50% of the bonuses are based on the score of a TAP-created observational rubric (conducted 3–6 times per year), and 50% are based on a value-added score of student achievement. For teachers with an established classroom of students, 30% of the bonus is based on their individual classroom growth and 20% on schoolwide growth. For teachers and other school personnel without an established classroom, the schoolwide growth accounts for their 50% of the value-added score.

Counter to the Denver Public Schools evaluation, this TAP evaluation found significant achievement effects for elementary school students and limited or no effects for middle and high school students. Glazerman and Seifullah (2010) also examined the impacts of the TAP program for eight schools in Chicago and found no significant differences in achievement after the first year of the program.

SUMMARY OF EVIDENCE

The evaluations of merit pay programs illustrate the wide range of bonuses offered, the varied employees eligible for bonuses, and the manner and criteria by which teachers/school personnel are able to earn these bonuses. The variation in these program components makes the evaluations and impact of the programs difficult to synthesize into a single statement about their effectiveness, which is perhaps one of the reasons the debate over merit pay persists. Further, each of the evaluations also varies in its rigor and clarity of findings and limitations, which makes specific statements about the expectations of such a program difficult.

Considering the evidence in total and recognizing the varying quality of evaluations, we conclude that the preponderance of evidence does generally report positive impacts for teacher attitudes and school culture. For student achievement, many studies find no significant difference or a small difference, but a difference. Recognizing that not all the evaluations are conducted with the same level of rigor or purpose, we provide more weight to those with more rigorous approaches in their design and analysis.

The results of two recent rigorous studies—the Nashville study (Springer, Ballou, et al., 2010) and the New York City study (Fryer, 2011)—call into question the motivation theory of merit pay. That is, these results suggest that the types of merit pay plans initiated in New York and Nashville are not likely to be effective in moving teacher quality or student achievement in the short term. However, these short-term studies do not address the question of whether the introduction of a meaningful merit-based component to teacher compensation might foster a positive change in the composition of the teacher workforce.

Overall, the evidence base suggests that we should not expect the adoption of merit pay programs (of the types used up to this point) to lead to short-term gains in student achievement. However, some of the programs reviewed above show promising results, and some of the ineffective programs may well have been poorly designed. Thus, we believe there is still merit in developing—and carefully evaluating—programs that introduce performance-based compensation for education. Moreover, because many policymakers and practitioners continue to look for productive ways to move beyond the single-salary system for teachers, it is imperative that we consider the results of previous programs in building new ones. Indeed, in some cases, our review of the evidence showed us what not to do! Throughout the rest of this book, then, the information provided within this chapter is referenced and gleaned to provide a step-by-step approach to developing a plan.

To expand on the current research base discussed in this chapter, we also draw from our own experiences in developing compensation reform strategies. We have collectively developed a host of different proposals, including discussions with legislators across multiple states and at the federal level. We have worked extensively with district personnel, state departments, and outside agencies to create different plans aimed at the needs of the local communities, all of which center on recruiting and retaining more effective educators.

However, consistent with the literature discussed above, even with our combined efforts and the recognition of the available literature on merit pay, we have not yet produced a program that shows consistent gains for students. Notwithstanding, our resolve is firmly rooted in the theory and promising gains made in understanding what can work when all the pieces fit together.

Primarily, we are optimistic about the use of compensation reform due to the known problems with the current system. The existing educator compensation system is knowingly insufficient in drawing additional high-caliber applicants into the field and retaining them once in the field. There are obvious perverse incentives inherent in the single-salary system that discourage innovation and limit the ability of school leaders to retain the most effective teachers and deploy these teachers where they are needed most. Thoughtful teacher compensation reform can address these issues. Further, compensation reform connected to performance objectives can support ongoing efforts in professional development and can encourage educators to work as a cohesive team.

Before we provide the framework for a plan guided by our experiences and literature, the next chapter lays the foundation for this journey by examining and responding to key criticisms of merit pay using the aforementioned evidence and our own experiences with teachers and school leaders.

4

The Top 12 Criticisms of Merit Pay

1. Merit pay would unfairly reward the teachers of the brightest students and further discourage teachers from working with low-performing students.

2. The use of merit pay will further encourage the unhealthy strategy of "teaching to the test."

3. Teachers did not enter this field for the money, so why would money influence them?

4. Teacher merit is too hard to measure.

5. Merit pay ratings are each based on their own "secret formula" that is not at all meaningful or motivational to most teachers.

6. Teachers are already working as hard as they can, and this will not change behavior.

7. Merit pay programs generally offer rewards of $3,000 or less; this is not enough to make a difference.

8. "Weighing the pig is not going to make it any fatter"—or how is measuring teacher effectiveness supposed to make teachers better?

9. Merit pay would be entirely irrelevant to educators who do not teach non-core subjects and would serve to devalue subjects such as art, foreign language, and physical education.

10. While merit pay may have been a consideration during better financial times, state policymakers cannot afford to implement such expensive plans during times of fiscal crisis (such as in 2012).

11. Merit pay programs lead to counterproductive competition among teachers and discourage collegiality.

12. No evidence proves merit pay works.

Throughout this chapter, we will outline each of these 12 concerns and discuss strategies program developers could adopt to address each. Most of these criticisms are based on legitimate issues that should inform plan developers as they put together the details of teacher merit pay plans. In the end, we will conclude that infant plans stand a better chance of being effective if they are built in a way that is attentive to the legitimate concerns of merit pay critics.

The reader may also notice that we have framed these criticisms as definitive and factual. That is, "merit pay causes . . ." or "merit pay discourages . . ." or "merit pay will . . . ." While we intentionally framed the criticisms in this way, there is of course no certainty around these issues. Moreover, remember that no single or uniform plan called "merit pay" exists. That is, teacher merit pay plans can be designed in numerous ways in various settings; thus, we should be skeptical of merit pay critics highlighting exactly what merit pay programs will do or will cause or not do or not cause. Indeed, our fundamental point in this chapter is to identify the legitimate concerns of merit pay critics and discuss the issues that must be considered and the challenges that must be overcome in building a plan that has the best chance of success.

If we are not talking about the details of the plan, we cannot intelligently assess which components of plans are connected to the desired outcomes. Merit pay is a broad concept that can and does take on various forms, but the devil is in the details. So, for those who are building plans and thinking about the details, here are some "devils" that should be considered!

1. MERIT PAY DISCOURAGES TEACHING DISADVANTAGED STUDENTS

> *I fear that instituting a merit pay system may encourage teaching to the test and discourage teachers from working in schools with large numbers of disadvantaged students.*
>
> —Senator Christopher Dodd (All American Patriots, 2007)

This genuine concern is voiced by many who publicly oppose merit pay for teachers. Dennis Van Roekel, president of the National Education Association, argued, "With merit pay, there would be no incentive for me to teach Basic Math, but every incentive to teach Calculus." His reasoning, of course, was that he believed that "there is a greater chance that my Calculus students will score higher on a standardized test" ("Issue Clash," 2009).

Seasoned researchers David Berliner and Gene Glass have voiced similar concerns. Professor Glass (1995) describes a scenario in which two teachers are assigned classes with very different overall ability levels, and these differences are demonstrated through a high-quality assessment measure at the start of the school year. Then, these two equally talented teachers put forth similar effort and teach at the top of their abilities throughout the year. Glass concludes, quite reasonably, that the higher ability class of students will score better on the posttest at the end of the school year.

Based on situations such as this, Berliner concludes, "I think we'll find that most of the rewards will go to the affluent schools. Most of the punishments will go to schools with the harder-to-teach kids" (Scherer, 2001, p. 9).

This point is critically important and one that we agree with in circumstances where a substantial portion of a merit program is based on year-end achievement scores only; there would indeed be perverse incentives. Such plans would likely provide further encouragement for teachers to shy away from low-performing students and seek out their easier-to-teach peers. In such cases, we would call this a poorly designed merit pay plan.

Consequently, plan developers should insist that teacher ratings be based on student academic growth and teacher performance growth throughout the school year rather than on year-end, student achievement levels. Merit pay rating systems focused on student improvement will not encourage teachers to abandon struggling students. Moreover, teacher performance and even student performance rating systems could be designed such that gains from low-achieving students are weighted more heavily than gains from other students. In this way, *school leaders could build merit pay plans that encourage their best teachers to seek out disadvantaged students and then reward such teachers for moving these students forward.*

Again, the key to this argument is that "merit pay" is not a singular, monolithic policy but one that should and must be tailored to fit the school's needs. And the best people to determine that are those at the school.

2. MERIT PAY ENCOURAGES TEACHING TO THE TEST

> *I don't know where I would be today if my teachers' job security was based on how I performed on some standardized test. If their very survival as teachers was based not on whether I actually fell in love with the process of learning but rather if I could fill in the right bubble on a test. If they had to spend most of their time desperately drilling us and less time encouraging creativity and original ideas; less time knowing who we were, seeing our strengths and helping us realize our talents.*
>
> —Actor Matt Damon, August 1, 2011, at a Save Our Schools rally in Washington, D.C.

With the passage of No Child Left Behind in 2002, there has been an increased focus on the results of standardized tests and increases in the amount of time allocated to standardized exams. Students in most states sit for 10 to 15 hours of standardized assessments per year (Ritter & Holley, 2008). While students still spend very few hours taking standardized exams, many have claimed that the enhanced importance of these assessments (which are used for accountability purposes in many states) has resulted in problems associated with "teaching to the test." If implemented, merit pay plans would only enhance the importance of student testing. Thus, if teaching to the test were genuinely a problem, the negative repercussions would likely increase with the implementation of merit pay plans.

While there is no agreed-on definition of this popular term, opponents of testing have drawn the connection between increased testing and negative outcomes in classrooms. First, critics allege that increased testing, along with consequences for performance, can lead to systematic cheating on standardized exams. We will not focus on this concern, as we believe that most students and educators engage in test-taking of various kinds during each and every school year and do so with integrity. Despite a few high-profile cheating scandals, we do not view this as a widespread problem (and, if it were a widespread problem, the implications would go well beyond the decision to implement a merit pay program for teachers and is thus outside of our aims in this guide).

More mainstream concerns are that any enhanced focus on standardized testing might encourage educators to

- focus too much on test-prep skills,
- narrow the curriculum to focus almost exclusively on tested subjects, or

- tone down their creativity and choose to engage the students in rote memorization.

These are important concerns and worthy of consideration. First of all, while numerous anecdotes suggest that schools are engaging in test preparation, there is no systematic evidence to support this claim. Similarly, while there are anecdotes of schools that are limiting the study of subjects outside of reading and math, there is not a strong base of evidence supporting this claim. Certainly, we would not recommend that educators engage in narrowing the curriculum in this way. One of the best ways to become a better reader, for example, and thus prepare for reading tests, is to study a wide range of academic subjects (such as history, art, etc.).

Finally, while it is easy to dig up quotes from educators who believe that their creativity is stifled by state tests, it is not obvious that the existence of standardized assessments should encourage teachers to be less creative. In fact, students who are taught by engaging and creative teachers focusing on the appropriate material are likely to do just fine on most assessments of student learning, standardized or otherwise.

In most states, policymakers have come to an agreement as to what children ought to be learning in each grade and subject, and have developed assessments designed to test those skills and subjects. In this context, it would seem that the role of the teacher is to teach a broad range of academic content that is reflective of the relevant standards. The movement toward national frameworks, or the Common Core State Standards, further suggests that the role of standards is not inherently bad. In fact, providing guidance for each grade level can help provide both veteran, expert teachers and incoming, novice teachers with a sense of how to connect their teaching to that of the grade below and that above. In our view, focusing on content that will happen to be tested is not the same as "gaming" the test. Rather, if we assume the tests are fairly examining what we have decided children ought to learn, then "teaching to the test" actually means little more than teaching.

In the context of merit pay, it seems appropriate to argue that those teachers who accomplish this task especially effectively should be given fittingly high ratings. Nevertheless, there are several lessons to be drawn here for school leaders considering the adoption of a merit pay plan. First of all, any assessments that will form the basis for teacher ratings must be clearly connected to the goals of the school and district. Second, rating systems should not be based solely on test scores, since teachers focus on many important goals, not all of which can be measured by student achievement gains on exams.

3. WHAT ABOUT TEACHERS OF NONTESTED SUBJECTS?

> *Currently, fewer than half of all public school teachers teach a tested subject in a tested grade. . . . In addition, there's the thorny question of whether it's fair to evaluate and pay a math teacher according to "objective" test-score data, while relying on a highly subjective portfolio system to evaluate and pay an art teacher.*
>
> —Dana Goldstein (2011), Spencer Education Journalism Fellow at Columbia University

It is certainly true that merit plans work the best for teachers of, for example, middle school math, because students in these grades are tested annually in this subject. Thus, without any additional testing, school leaders can gather an estimate of student learning gains during the school year. For teachers of other subjects, estimating their contributions to student learning can be a bit more complicated.

Nonetheless, the fact that allocating merit ratings and merit pay to non-core teachers presents some unique challenges does not render merit pay unworkable. Rather, program developers will need to devise other strategies to rate these specialist teachers or school support staff.

In some programs, these teachers who cannot reasonably be directly connected with test score gains for discrete sets of students receive the bulk of their merit ratings based on schoolwide student achievement or student achievement growth. The positive aspect of this strategy is that all teachers are working together toward a common goal. On the other hand, such a group-based goal structure can encourage the free-rider problem, whereby individual participants do not take responsibility for pursuing the group's goals because they can benefit from the efforts of others. An additional problematic feature of such a plan is that individuals within the school may well feel that they do not have control over their own merit rewards. That is, even if they work very diligently and effectively, this effort has only a marginal effect on schoolwide achievement. Thus, teachers of non-core subjects may perceive (correctly) that they have little influence over their own merit rewards. Of course, the motivational impact of a merit pay program will be minimal if participants do not believe their efforts will be duly rewarded.

An alternate strategy—one that we will explore in more detail in the description of an example program in Chapter 7—is to allow more subjective and personalized ratings to be given to teachers whose own goals are more subjective in nature. For example, the fine arts teacher might be rated, in large part, on the extent to which his or her students succeed in fine arts competitions (if this is, indeed, an objective within the fine arts program). The physical education teacher and football coach might be rated on the academic achievement growth of players on the football team, if one of the goals of the football program is to develop student athletes. Such a strategy would be time-consuming in that the principal would need to develop annual, and somewhat measurable, goals in cooperation with each non-core faculty member. Nonetheless, this time-consuming process would likely be useful in itself in that it would mandate annual discussions of teacher goals and progress toward those goals.

4. MERIT PAY ASSUMES THAT TEACHERS TEACH FOR THE MONEY; THEY DON'T!

> *One of the signature issues of businesspeople and conservative Republicans for the past 30 years has been merit pay. . . . Note that they assume that most people—in this case, teachers—are lazy and need a promise of dollars to be incentivized to get higher scores for their students. It never seems to occur to them that many people are doing their best (think people who play sports, always striving to do their best without any expectation of payment) and continue to do so because of intrinsic rewards or because of an innate desire to serve others. Teachers should certainly be well compensated, but not many enter the classroom with money as their primary motivation.*
>
> —Education Researcher Diane Ravitch (Strauss, 2010)

This assumption is a common theme in the merit pay discussion. Teachers are not concerned about money, the argument goes, or else they would never have entered the field of teaching. This concern seems plausible on its face. Teachers have indeed entered a field in which the pay scales are set and there are few opportunities for substantial financial rewards. Additionally, teachers often need to work for a number of years before gaining access to their retirement funds—something not considered by many young adults as they enter the field but nonetheless an important piece of the financial "pie."

However, it is incorrect to say that, by virtue of choosing teaching, teachers have revealed that they do not care about financial rewards. Different teachers, of course, have different options in the labor market. For some teachers, this option was the highest paying option available. These teachers may have chosen this profession for the money. Others may have felt the "calling" to be a teacher and never gave serious thought to any other career option. In most cases, teachers (and other employees) consider the various types of "compensation" a job offers and weigh this compensation when choosing whether or not to take a job. Teaching, like many other jobs, offers an array of benefits that include base salary, health benefits, job security, working hours, flexibility, and enjoyment. For most teachers, some aspects of the compensation package are attractive (e.g., good benefits, high levels of job security, and working hours that include summer breaks) and other aspects are less attractive (e.g., base salary, a lack of flexibility during the school day).

In any event, it is clear that teachers do care, to some extent, about the compensation they receive for their work. Teachers go on strike for numerous reasons, including higher salaries (consider the 2012 Chicago teacher strike), and teacher openings with higher salaries generally attract more interest than those with lower salaries. In North Carolina, for example, hundreds of teachers across the state contacted lawmakers to protest a 30% cut in annual teacher performance bonuses for the 2007–2008 school year (teachers in schools that showed high growth received bonuses of $1,053 instead of $1,500 as expected). Not surprisingly, most teachers, like most people, prefer more money to less money and enjoy being recognized for doing good work.

We are also aware of the research that suggests there are numerous characteristics of the working environment that matter more than money to teachers. For example, *teachers prefer supportive leadership, parents who reinforce school learning, some autonomy, and pleasant working conditions.* We agree that these job attributes are important and positions in schools that are more favorable on these scores will be more likely to attract good teachers. However, the challenge is that these job traits are likely not as easily manipulated by policy as is teacher pay. That is, it is difficult to imagine a law or policy that would immediately result in supportive leadership, for example. Conversely, policymakers can implement merit pay with the stroke of a pen. This is an important point and a reason why merit pay is advancing as a policy to address some of the disparities we see in America's educational system.

Last, we should keep in mind that the "teachers don't care about money" criticism focuses only on those who have already decided to enter teaching. In fact, many merit pay proponents believe the greatest potential benefit of this reform is the possibility that teaching may become attractive to some who chose not to pursue teaching in the past. Specifically, more research on the reasons why high achievers do not enter the teaching field finds that resources do matter for these students. In 2006, Breglio began asking top students characteristics of their ideal jobs. Students from the University of Southern California and the University of California–Los Angeles listed four key attributes of their ideal jobs. The most important characteristic was good money/great pay.

In the end, of all the oft-cited criticisms of merit pay, this may be the least important and the most easily dismissed, as we can agree that teachers do not all teach for the money, but they *do* get paid to teach and should be compensated for doing good work.

5. TEACHER MERIT IS JUST TOO HARD TO MEASURE

> *I was once bullish on the idea of using "value-added methods" for assessing teacher effectiveness. I have since realized that these measures, while valuable for large-scale studies, are seriously flawed for evaluating individual teachers, and that rigorous, ongoing assessment by teaching experts serves everyone better.*
>
> —Education Researcher Linda Darling-Hammond (2012)

While much of this debate is politicized and polarized, with people on both sides digging in their heels and closing their minds to any discussion, others believe that a valid form of teacher evaluation is sorely needed but are not sure if the tools are yet available. Today, many testing experts and education policy analysts are studying and debating the extent to which value-added measures are fair representations of teacher effectiveness (see Amrein-Beardsley, 2012; Harris, 2011).

Simply put, value-added indicators attempt to measure the value that each individual teacher adds to the learning of his or her students during a given time period. To be clear, work still needs to be done on value-added measures, and throughout this guide, we advocate for multiple measures from multiple sources (including teacher knowledge, teacher performance, collegiality, and student achievement measures). Nevertheless, it seems clear that value-added measures represent a real improvement over simple reviews of year-end student test scores, and over current teacher evaluation policies that do not pay any attention to student achievement.

Generally speaking, most systems of merit pay for individual teachers rely on the ability of a selected value-added measure to separate the contribution of the teacher to student learning from all those other things (such as the prior learning of the student) the student already brings to the table. In their simplest forms, statistical value-added models can generate predicted year-end scores for each student based on individual characteristics and then rate teachers based on whether their students overperform or under-perform (see Harris, 2011, for a practitioner-friendly book on this topic).

Within the academic community, there is a lively debate over whether these value-added models are ready for prime time. Statistical prediction models such as these are never perfect and clearly represent an estimate of each teacher's contribution to student learning. The shortcomings of such models are recognized by all (or nearly all, as even the developers of most value-added metrics note that they should not be relied on solely for employment decisions). The question, however, is whether these estimates are appropriate to use as part of a teacher evaluation scheme. For those interested in digging into the academic minutiae, two interesting pieces that sum up the two sides of the debate were published in the wake of the highly publicized decision by the *Los Angeles Times* to publish individual value-added scores for teachers in the Los Angeles schools.

On the heels of this publication, the Economic Policy Institute, in August 2010, convened a well-known group of researchers and testing experts who published a report titled "Problems With the Use of Student Test Scores to Evaluate Teachers" (Rothstein et al., 2010). The group concluded, in short, that student test scores are not reliable indicators of teacher effectiveness. In response, the Brookings Brown Center Task Group on Teacher Quality convened a group of noted statisticians and researchers who put out a report in 2010 arguing that, essentially, value added has an important role to play in teacher evaluation systems.

It is beyond the scope of this chapter to venture much more deeply into this debate. We are more persuaded by the argument that student achievement should be incorporated as one piece of a comprehensive teacher evaluation system and that value-added measures are an improvement over year-end comparisons. It is true that these measures contain errors and are not perfectly stable; thus, any high-stakes decisions based on these measures should account for the uncertainty. Small differences in value added should not lead to large differences in teacher ratings. Whenever possible, scores should be based on multiple years of data to minimize instability.

Most important, we must reiterate the counterfactual: value-added measures should not have to be perfect for policymakers to use them. Our current system of rating teachers, in which we do a very poor job of distinguishing between more and less effective teachers, is itself wildly imperfect. Policymakers must choose the best option from a set of imperfect options. In our view, a thoughtful rating system, and perhaps even a thoughtful merit pay system, is preferable to no rating system at all.

6. MERIT PAY RATINGS ARE BASED ON A SECRET FORMULA

> *Everything should be made as simple as possible, but not simpler.*
>
> —Paraphrase of Albert Einstein, 1900s

For a merit pay system, or any rating system, to serve as a motivator for participants, these same participants should have a clear understanding of what sorts of behaviors or outcomes will lead to positive ratings (and potentially rewards). Motivation theory suggests that employees are more likely to be motivated by reward systems when the goals are realistic and transparent.

Thus, school leaders should strive to create merit pay programs characterized by transparency and clarity, all else equal. However, all else is not equal. Increased clarity oftentimes comes at the cost of decreased sophistication or accuracy. For example, the current single-salary system is transparent and realistic—each year you work here, $500 is added to your base salary. However, as previously discussed, this system does little to motivate anyone to do more than simply continue showing up and is not connected to performance. On the other side, many merit pay programs incorporate a student achievement growth variable, which generally involves fairly complex statistical calculations.

Even these complicated models, however, could be employed to be more understandable to nonexperts. For example, the statistical models could be used to generate predicted year-end scores for each student. While nonexperts may not understand exactly how the predicted scores were generated, they would likely understand a spreadsheet that listed all students, their starting scores, and their predicted year-end scores. These lists would make intuitive sense to the teachers, as they would illustrate, generally, that students with relatively high pre-scores would have higher predicted year-end scores. In a plan such as this, teacher ratings based on the extent to which students score above or below their predicted scores would fit within their existing classroom goals and provide targets for most teachers. Additionally, as such programs become more common, more teachers will become familiar with the programs. Later, we discuss different programs that are more or less parsimonious and the value of including more or fewer measures of effectiveness.

In any event, school leaders should carefully consider the trade-off between transparency and sophistication and consult with representatives of the faculty in deciding on measures of teacher effectiveness.

The primary takeaway from this section is that teacher merit evaluations should not be "black box" or "secret" in nature. If the teachers and/or staff of the school have not understood the program (whether they vote for it or it is implemented without a vote), then the program will have reduced chances of success. The responsibility of the administration is to make certain their educators understand how they will be evaluated. With greater levels of buy-in from the teachers come better chances for program success.

7. TEACHERS ARE ALREADY WORKING AS HARD AS THEY CAN

> *It is surprising what a man can do when he has to, and how little most men will do when they don't have to.*
>
> —Walter Linn

Perhaps one reason that some educators bristle at the idea of merit pay is the implication that teachers are not currently giving maximum effort. Some in the field have viewed merit pay proposals as an indictment of "lazy" teachers. While we understand that this particular stance causes some of the kneejerk rejections of merit pay, we attempt to analyze this question objectively. To begin, we must recognize that there are more than 3 million teachers in America's education system, including exceptionally gifted, regular, and bad teachers. Virtually any principal, and likely most teachers, can identify at least one colleague who they know is not helping students. We need to be honest about this concept to devise policies aimed at improving education holistically, including the improvement of the most important piece in the puzzle—teachers.

Recognizing how important teachers are and that some are undervalued (meaning they are working much harder than those around them with no tangible benefit) and some are overvalued (meaning they are working far less than others and receiving the same tangible benefits), we seek ways to reward and encourage those who are giving their all and to discourage those who are inclined to "just get by."

Teachers, like all other professionals, value many things and are balancing many preferences. Teachers like doing a good job, helping students, earning money, and spending time with their families. Generally speaking, teachers—again, like other professionals—are giving only a portion of their attention to their job because they have other interests and priorities. Thus, we do believe that, for most teachers and most employees in any profession, there likely is some available room for them to increase their efforts.

However, as we noted in the first chapter, we contend that this issue is more complicated than simple increases in effort. For example, many teachers likely put forth great effort and are excellent at engaging students and delivering compelling lessons; however, those teachers may not have invested energy to ensure that these lessons are aligned with the district's or state's curricula. While courses taught by this teacher may be engaging and interesting, they may not build the foundational skills students need for the years that follow. In the absence of any external motivation, the teacher may feel comfortable focusing on whatever content he or she deems important, rather than on the content required in the state or district curricular guidelines.

In such instances, merit pay plans connected to the students' mastery of the school's "standards" will most certainly encourage teachers to pursue the school's mission by focusing on the curricular guidelines. Economist Ed Lazear (2003) agrees and suggests that "tying compensation to the appropriate metric provides incentives to move in the direction that has been agreed on" (p. 182). Thus, merit pay advocates hope that school leaders may use pay to motivate some teachers to work harder but also to encourage some otherwise excellent teachers to work *differently,* by ensuring that they give consideration to the agreed-on curricular standards when developing their lessons.

Even more fundamentally, we realize that most of us are balancing the many priorities we have, both at our workplace and away from our workplace. And we place different priorities (or levels of urgency) on different tasks that require our attention based on the consequences associated with each task. The greater the consequences attached, the more effort we will likely give a task. Thus, it seems reasonable that increasing the consequences attached to student understanding of state curricular standards will encourage teachers to put more effort toward pursuing this objective.

Of course, this is going to occur only in merit pay plans in which the goals of a program are clearly articulated and aligned with the standards they are pursuing. Additionally, teachers need to believe that increased effort can lead to positive consequences for students and that the teachers will, in turn, be rated positively for this increased effort and effectiveness.

Consider the Teacher Advancement Program (TAP) of the National Institute for Excellence in Teaching. This program provides teachers with evaluations four to six times per year (rather than the nearly useless drive-by reviews some teachers receive once a year), using a standardized rubric. The evaluations are both announced and unannounced and conducted by multiple trained and certified evaluators using the TAP *Teaching Skills, Knowledge and Responsibilities Performance Standards.* According to the program guidelines, before the announced evaluations, the evaluators and teachers meet for a preconference to discuss the upcoming evaluation. Then, following the evaluation, a postconference session is conducted between the observed teacher and the evaluator to discuss reinforcements and refinements intended to help the teacher strengthen his or her instructional practice (Eckert, 2009).

The old adage "work smarter, not harder" comes to mind. As noted earlier, we believe most teachers are working hard, putting their all into a highly demanding and intrinsically rewarding profession. We're not advocating for more hours to be spent or for more time to be given per se (unless it should be, which each person needs to determine). However, merit pay plans can be useful to the extent that they allow school leaders to provide guidance on school or district areas of priority; this seems like a reasonable strategy to help teachers know where to put their time and energy. Such efforts allow the teachers to have a plan of how to "work smarter" by refining their practice based on clear structure and feedback, as opposed to reacting to general comments such as, "You should work harder," which do little to help or motivate and are all too common in our current system.

8. MERIT PAY BONUSES ARE TOO SMALL TO MATTER

> *Money is better than poverty, if only for financial reasons.*
>
> —Woody Allen

Past merit pay plans have been criticized for asking for a great deal from the teachers in return for relatively small rewards. Rational teachers (and all persons) will consider pursuing a bonus if the value of the bonus is substantial and the likelihood of meeting the goal is reasonably high. If the teacher does not expect the value of the bonus to exceed the effort required to reach the goal, that teacher is probably not going to be motivated by the potential bonus.

Nevertheless, many merit pay plans are based on bonus levels that are comparatively small and thus unlikely to motivate any change in behavior or effort. For example, Texas's District Awards for Teacher Excellence program resulted in average bonuses of just over $1,000 per teacher. The well-known North Carolina teacher bonus plan offered a maximum award of $1,500 per teacher in the most effective schools and $750 for teachers in schools that "met expectations." It is simply hard to imagine a teacher, or anyone, putting forth a great deal of effort, trying new instructional strategies, or working much harder for the *chance* to earn $1,500 six months from now!

Despite this obvious weakness of low-value teacher bonus programs, schools continue to employ these, presumably in an attempt to stretch the finite bonus pool to be shared with as many teachers as possible. In our view, if the budget does not allow for substantial awards (e.g., at least 15% of the average teacher's salary) to be offered to effective teachers, school leaders should not go through the considerable effort required to build faculty consensus and develop the details of a plan. The central point of this issue is that small bonuses can actually do harm to motivating anyone. Indeed, the implementation of a plan with small bonuses might actually do harm to the school environment if the development of the plan unsettles the faculty and the potential rewards attached to the plan are not substantial enough to generate teacher buy-in.

9. HOW IS MEASURING TEACHER EFFECTIVENESS SUPPOSED TO IMPROVE INSTRUCTION?

> *You don't make a pig fatter by weighing it.*
>
> —Anonymous

There is some concern that teacher compensation reform has no underlying theory of change. The simple theory of action, critics complain, is that school leaders will begin to measure performance of teachers and better align financial consequences with performance, and then teachers will magically perform better without any other changes or supports provided to them.

In our view, this criticism is legitimate to a number of merit pay plans. Although neither of us are animal experts, we certainly believe that the act of weighing a pig does not in and of itself "fatten" the pig. However, the pig represents an imperfect analogy to the merit pay situation. First of all, in the case of the pig, we might not need a scale to figure out if the pig needs fattening; we can assess this with our own eyes. On the other hand, we cannot simply judge with our eyes whether teachers are effective. So, the simple act of "weighing the pig," or assessing teacher effectiveness in improving student achievement, can be intrinsically useful for school leaders. Students would benefit if school leaders knew more about the relative effectiveness of teachers across the campus. It would be useful to know which teachers need additional specific professional development and which teachers should be leading that professional development.

While we believe there is value in measuring teacher effectiveness, we also suggest that merit pay plans will have a *better chance of success if coupled with more comprehensive school improvement strategies.* For example, school leaders implementing a merit pay plan may also want to implement better data sharing with teachers and professional development units aimed at helping teachers make the best use of student data in diagnosing student needs. Administrators need to identify and develop instructional leaders within the school. In order for the administrators to know how to obtain, design, and prescribe the appropriate development for certain teachers, they must also observe teachers more than once a year during a 5-minute window (or by other minimally defined measures). Simply evaluating teachers and indicating a value-added score and then providing them with some amount of resources will do little to encourage change or engender support for the program.

Previously, we described TAP, which requires four to six different evaluations per year conducted by different evaluators who are trained and certified to conduct these evaluations. The evaluators then meet with the teachers and discuss the evaluation, which also includes a videotaped segment of their teaching that they review together. These types of evaluations, which are also akin to those used by the National Board for Professional Teaching Standards candidacy exams, have the potential to lead to much better programs.

As discussed throughout this chapter and on this point in particular, the skepticism voiced by some critics that evaluation or merit pay alone will lead to improved teaching seems reasonable in our view. District and school leaders must ensure that evaluations and merit pay plans are developed within a frame of improvement and identification for areas of improvement. Then the financial bonuses exist as rewards for those who successfully advance on those goals.

10. MERIT PAY ENCOURAGES COUNTERPRODUCTIVE COMPETITION AND DISCOURAGES COLLEGIALITY

There is a well-established, substantial body of educational research that has found individual merit pay for teachers fails to produce meaningful gains in student achievement. What is more, individual merit pay has negative consequences, as the culture of trust and collaboration that is at the heart of a good school is undermined when educators are set in invidious competition with one another.

—Leo Casey, vice president for Academic High Schools, United Federation of Teachers ("Is the Merit Pay Debate Settled?" 2011)

This criticism is perhaps the most common voiced by ardent critics of any type of teacher merit pay. Dennis Van Roekel, president of the National Education Association, argued, "Merit pay systems force teachers to compete, rather than cooperate. They create a disincentive for teachers to share information and teaching techniques" ("Issue Clash," 2009). Teacher unions have historically based their opposition to merit pay on this key issue. Collaboration and teamwork among teachers is viewed by many as a core principle of the teaching profession. Indeed, if we imagine the faculty lounge in an ideal school, the teachers would spend time together informally discussing teaching strategies and student needs. Moreover, this school would provide numerous opportunities for formal interactions in which teachers work together to improve in their craft.

This is another fundamental concern, and we would certainly agree that merit pay plans *could* include components that discourage collaboration among teachers. However, as we noted above, numerous design options and merit pay plans could (and should) be built to *encourage* collaboration among faculty. And in our view, this is a critically important detail that school leaders consider as they design a plan. The fear that poorly designed merit pay plans will create unhealthy competition among teachers is a legitimate one, particularly with any plan that divides a fixed amount of reward dollars among a set number of teachers.

We do not recommend such "zero-sum" plans and instead recommend that plans foster collaboration in the two following ways:

First, plans should be built to rate teachers and allocate awards to teachers based on the extent to which they meet their individually set goals, regardless of how other teachers perform. Thus, one teacher's likelihood of meeting his or her goals is not negatively affected when another teacher meets his or her goal. This creates a far better situation than one that pits teachers against one another.

Second, a collaborative program design will go one step further by incorporating within the teacher rating a team-based or schoolwide component. In this way, the "merit" rating for classroom teachers with tested students should be based, in part, on groupwide or schoolwide student achievement growth. In this type of plan, teachers benefit both from the achievement growth of students in their own classrooms *and* from the achievement growth of all students.

Thus, while this criticism is reasonable and thoughtful, it is not damning of the entire concept of merit pay. To be proactive in this concern, *school leaders could build merit pay plans that reward teachers for schoolwide growth and encourage teachers to collaborate, discuss student needs, and share instructional strategies.*

A clear theme is emerging from these legitimate criticisms that we have discussed before. Merit pay is not a singular idea. There is no "merit pay plan," just as there is no single way to teach multiplication. However, there are better and worse components to use within such plans, and we continue to see that when plans are developed thoughtfully, these issues can be addressed.

11. STATES CAN'T AFFORD MERIT PAY DURING TIMES OF FISCAL AUSTERITY

> *The budget situation was a challenge and necessary cuts had to be made.*
>
> —Catherine Frazier, a spokeswoman for Texas Governor Rick Perry (Stutz, 2011)

This concern become even more salient in mid-2011 when policymakers in Texas, a state that had embraced merit pay like no other, decided to cut funding to the largest teacher merit pay program in the nation by 90%. Budget concerns are obviously very important for local policymakers. We have spoken to many school leaders who are intrigued with the idea of a merit pay plan but are unable (or unwilling) to adopt any new programs when resources are perceived to be tighter than normal.

Indeed, much of the growth in merit pay plans over the past 5 years or so has been driven by federal Teacher Incentive Fund awards, which have given districts and states the political cover and the necessary funds to adopt controversial merit pay plans. There are fewer examples of local districts (or states) that supported teacher merit pay plans out of local funds. So, based on past experience, we should not expect local policymakers to begin to allocate a substantial fraction of local budgets toward this type of teacher compensation reform.

However, it is also possible that the fiscal crises affecting policymakers at statehouses across the country may bode well for merit pay reforms. Given that resources may be tighter than normal in many state budgets, state policymakers may be unable to provide the standard pay raises teachers are accustomed to receiving each year. In this case, we could imagine policymakers striking a deal with teacher leaders in which policymakers scour the budgets for funding for salary increases and teacher leaders agree that these increases be allocated based on merit.

This type of compromise is not without precedent in the world of education. In the late 1990s and early 2000s in many states, policymakers increased school funding levels and school leaders accepted the imposition of greater levels of accountability in return for the increased funding. Similarly, in the next several years, we may see policymakers and teacher leaders arriving at a similar compromise, and the result could be a proliferation of teacher merit pay programs, where teacher groups can garner the raises they seek but in the form of bonuses attached to improved teacher practices and improved student outcomes.

12. MERIT PAY IS AN UNPROVEN REFORM

> *Merit pay comes in many forms and flavors. . . . We've looked at dozens of plans in North America, South America, Asia, Europe, and the Middle East. Guess what? None of them, past and present, has ever had a successful track record. None has ever produced its intended results. Any gains have been minimal, short-lived, and expensive to achieve.*
>
> —Vivian Troen and Katherine C. Boles (2005)

This argument has gained momentum, particularly after results from Tennessee and New York were released in 2010 and 2011. The results of the National Center on Performance Initiatives Nashville study (Springer, Ballou, et al., 2010) and of the New York City RAND study (Fryer, 2011) certainly call into question the motivation theory of merit pay and the potential short-term results. We would caution, however, due to a variety of weaknesses in the designs of these two particular plans, that it is still too early to close the book on the possibility that a well-designed merit pay scheme could result in enhanced teacher motivation in the short term. More important, however, these sobering findings from two short-term programs provide no insight into the potential benefits that the broader adoption of merit pay might foster for the overall composition of the teaching force. In our current non-merit-pay world, newly entering teachers can expect very high levels of job security but very few rewards for high performance.

This recipe may not be appealing to talented young people confident that they would flourish in a more differentiated system. The data agree: Unfortunately, on average, our most talented college graduates do not aspire to be teachers (Teach for America is one notable exception). However, if teacher salaries were related to effectiveness, talented and self-assured individuals might be more likely to enter the profession and turn into excellent classroom teachers.

Indeed, the widespread use of merit pay has the potential to enhance the composition of the teaching corps at the front end and beyond. Over time, a well-designed merit pay system would send the right signals and foster a sort of "natural selection" whereby effective teachers, encouraged by annual recognition and rewards, would eagerly return to the classroom each year. At the same time, their less effective peers would find teaching to be less financially rewarding and would thus work to improve their skills or seek out other career options.

Perhaps the greatest hope of merit pay advocates is that the introduction of a meaningful merit-based component to teacher compensation might foster a systematic change by which more talented individuals are attracted to teaching, excellent teachers remain in the classroom, and those who are not suited to the profession seek a new career. On this point, we have only logic and intuition—but no studies—to guide us.

Furthermore, what if we turned the question on its head? *That is, what is the evidence that the current system of uniform pay scales with lock-step salary increases is optimal?* Of course, we would find there is no evidence supporting this strategy either, but we continue it. Thus, if we truly want to use evidence of effectiveness as our deciding factor, it appears to be a tie! Again, since the evidence does not yet point in a clear direction on this question, perhaps we should appeal to logic.

The objective of this chapter is to address criticisms often leveled against those seeking ways to adjust the compensation structure of educators. Throughout this chapter, we acknowledge some of the legitimate concerns of merit pay opponents and consider how to use those concerns as a useful guide in developing plans. In responding to these common criticisms, we uncovered a set of useful guidelines to ensure that those developing merit pay plans could avoid the common pitfalls. These principles are detailed in the next chapter, and we believe they must be addressed for merit pay plans to have a chance of being successful in rewarding and retaining effective teachers while serving as recruiting tools for talented teacher prospects.

5

Guiding Principles and Pesky Questions

In the previous chapter, we highlighted the concerns of critics of merit pay as issues that school leaders should consider in implementation of a teacher merit pay plan. In this chapter, we describe the overarching principles that we believe are essential for a merit pay program to be successful. Then, based on our experience and a thorough review of the relevant literature, we outline a set of questions that school leaders must thoughtfully consider and answer as they move through the process of developing a merit pay plan.

GUIDING PRINCIPLES FOR DESIGNING AND IMPLEMENTING A MERIT PAY PLAN

Merit pay plans have the best chance of gaining support and persisting if local stakeholders play a substantial role in tailoring the plan and developing many of the details. While local control is important, we do not believe every state or district must recreate the proverbial wheel regarding its evaluation and compensation system. Based on the lessons learned from other states and districts, there are a few guiding principles from which decision-makers should draw as a foundation for their work.

Principle 1: The Evaluation System Must Be Clear and Understandable

A key criticism of merit pay plans is that teachers view these plans as *secret formulas* and have no idea why merit bonuses were or were not awarded. If a merit pay plan is to successfully elicit excellent teaching, it must be based on a transparent payout scheme and a clear understanding of what kinds of outcomes the plan rewards. As we stated in the prior chapter, teachers must understand the goals that are set if we expect them to pursue these goals. These goals should be aligned with the district and/or state standards and, depending on the state, will potentially match the Common Core Standards currently being implemented across the nation.

The purpose of the "clear and understandable" evaluation system is that the teachers should be fully aware of what they are working toward, rather than simply being rewarded. Too often, merit pay plans are described as "black box" programs or "buddy system" programs, where teachers either do not know why they were rewarded or believe rewards were based on personal connections rather than objective standards. Clearly articulating the system can help reduce these types of criticisms once the program is operating.

One strategy we have employed in the past to make the program clear to the participants is the use of a "merit pay report card," which clearly outlines the teacher's areas of evaluation and the targets and results in each area. The merit pay ratings are based on a 100-point system (something quite familiar to most teachers), and the report cards clearly connect the "merit points" with the dollars earned for each teacher.

Principle 2: Consistent Communication Is Critical

School administrators and teachers should be involved at a very early stage, and all stakeholders must be kept informed throughout the process. One way school leaders can enhance communication is by forming a *merit pay exploratory committee* and then a *merit pay planning committee* (described in much more detail in the next chapter) comprising all types of faculty and school administrators. These committees should consistently and persistently work to keep teachers informed, at the onset of the plan and throughout the life of the plan.

As with attempting to implement any large-scale change, especially one related to money, any vacuum of information will likely be filled with provocative rumors, exaggerated claims, or outright falsehoods. On the other hand, if stakeholders know what is going on and know where to go for additional information, misinformation is less likely to be cultivated. Establishing clear lines of communication for disseminating any changes or questions will also allow for the system to be more seamlessly understood and, ultimately, far more effective.

Communication with participants is not only important at the outset of the program but also in the years that follow. We have firsthand experience of previously popular plans being derailed when program planners did not successfully communicate with program participants about changes in years 2 and 3. In fact, in our experience, the program changes in question were intended to benefit the faculty and make the rating system more clear; however, due to a lack of discussion around the issue, the prevailing sentiment among teacher participants was that the program staff were covertly making changes that would allow them to save money and pay lesser bonuses. While there was no truth to this allegation, the misinformation circulated easily among the ranks of the teachers with no resistance—even though the changes would actually result in larger bonuses.

Principle 3: Evaluations Should Be Based on Multiple and Thoughtful Measures of Effectiveness

It is clear that students have many needs and, thus, educators have many objectives. As a result, it would be silly to evaluate teachers on any single quantifiable measure; multiple measures are not only preferable but necessary. Moreover, all measures should be thoughtful and developed to create the appropriate incentives for educators; at the least, program planners should be careful to avoid perverse incentives. As an obvious example, teachers should not be evaluated on crude measures such as the fraction of students passing an arbitrary proficiency cutoff mark. Rather, educators should be rated based on *growth* in student achievement.

Even the staunchest advocates of standardized testing acknowledge that schools have goals that go beyond student achievement in "core" subjects.[1] Therefore, incorporating outcome measures beyond student achievement growth may provide a much more holistic evaluation system. But it could also make the system worse, depending on which measures are incorporated and how. Consequently, incorporating multiple measures should be done with careful planning and full information about the advantages and disadvantages of each measure being considered.

Specifically, some plans become too cumbersome to understand and undermine Principles 1 and 2 due to their diffused reward structure. The trade-off of comprehensive evaluation is also for complexity. Sometimes program developers are intimately familiar with data in the school and classroom; however, these data points are not always valuable criteria to put into an evaluation system of each teacher and may be used to determine the impact of the program rather than as a component of it.

---

[1] We put quotation marks around core because there is widespread debate among educators on what should be considered a core subject. We do not want to wade into the debate on core versus non-core subjects, as it falls outside the aim of our work in this book; however, we are discussing other policies already in place that require certain testing standards for different subjects.

Principle 4: Plans Should Actively Encourage Collaboration and Discourage Counterproductive Competition

Above all else—do no harm! That is, first and foremost, a merit pay plan should not foster divisiveness or unhealthy competition among a school's faculty. To ward off the possibility of unhealthy competition, avoid fixed-pot bonus plans based on relative rankings of teachers. If collaboration among teachers is desired (and, honestly, under what conditions would it *not* be?), then teachers shouldn't be fighting for limited spots in the bonus pool. Instead, each teacher's bonus should be based on his or her performance compared with his or her individual performance goals—in short, his or her students' and his or her own personal growth.

Moreover, a well-constructed plan can actually enhance teacher collaboration by incorporating group-based rewards in the merit pay plan. In this way, the good work of one teacher improves the rating of another; thus, teachers are all working toward the same goal to maximize student achievement while maximizing their bonuses at the same time. A portion of the non-achievement program could also be based on teacher collaboration as noted by the teachers themselves (i.e., nominating a lead teacher from each grade level to receive a bonus).

Principle 5: Merit Pay Plans Should Be Part of a Comprehensive School Improvement Strategy

One question often raised by critics relates to the "theory of action" of a merit pay strategy. That is, do the plan developers expect that teachers will simply choose to magically improve when money is placed on the table? While the motivating effect of the financial rewards is certainly part of the formula, the strategy may be more palatable to participants if implemented alongside other reforms that might foster school improvement.

One school improvement strategy that fits well with a merit pay plan is implementation of a formative assessment system that assesses student performance at multiple points throughout the school year. This strategy can foster a culture of data and continuous performance monitoring that enables teachers to identify individual students who needed assistance in particular areas or general areas where most students struggled. In this way, school leaders can provide teachers with additional tools to help raise student performance, in conjunction with financial rewards for improved effectiveness. An additional component of a comprehensive improvement plan is to connect professional development requirements to the evaluation system, which is connected to the state and/or district standards. Providing targeted and tailored professional development allows for a consistent message to be sent to all teachers and staff about the goals of the school and provides guidance for how these pieces fit together, rather than simply framing this instruction as "seat-time" sessions they need to retain certification.

Principle 6: Merit Pay Bonuses
Should Be Substantial and Meaningful

Research suggests that performance pay plans should feature substantial financial rewards for increases in student achievement. It is difficult to imagine that teachers would significantly alter their teaching approaches for a minimal bonus amount (such as a 1% raise, for instance). Small bonuses cannot be expected to promote increased effort in the classroom or to encourage teachers to try more innovative teaching strategies. For that reason, to be effective, a performance pay system should provide appropriate and substantial rewards for teachers who focus on improved student learning. We would suggest that teachers be given the chance to earn bonuses in the neighborhood of 15% of their annual salaries.

The six principles described above can serve as a useful foundation for the development and implementation of a merit pay plan. However, due to the general nature of these tenets, there is a great deal of flexibility and room for adaptation to local needs and preferences. As a first step in creating the local version of a merit pay plan, developers will need to begin to address several important questions focused on key details. In the next chapter, we describe a step-by-step timeline for program implementation, but we first outline a set of questions that must be answered in the process.

PESKY QUESTIONS

We group these questions into three broad categories. First, school leaders must identify which educators in the school or district will be invited to participate in the merit pay plan. The second set of questions relates to methods of measuring teacher effectiveness. The third set of questions involves translating these and other measures into systems of ratings and rewards. We have some preferred answers to these questions, which we share in the next chapter, where we present an example plan. In this chapter, however, we list many of the questions that must be answered without privileging one choice over another.

Identifying Program Participants

Perhaps the most fundamental question for designing a plan is, who will be eligible for an award? Some programs provide awards to teachers of "core" subjects with related standardized assessments; in other plans, non-core teachers and school support staff are eligible for awards, although the award levels and rating systems might be different. Other merit pay plans include awards for school administrators based on overall performance of the school or district. The necessity of establishing the participants for the program is that the structure of the evaluation, the amount of payouts, and the communication plan will all relate to who is involved. Specifically, program planners should address questions such as these:

- Which school employees will be eligible for the program?
- What categories of staff will be used for program purposes (e.g., core teachers of tested subjects, non-core teachers of special subjects such as art and physical education, school support staff such as receptionists, etc.)?
- Will school and/or district administrators participate in the merit pay program?

Measuring Teacher Effectiveness

When designing a teacher merit pay system, program developers also need to determine what measures of performance will be incorporated into the system. Teacher awards can be based on the level of student performance or value added, can be based on a discrete measure of student performance (such as proficiency) or on a continuous measure (such as a scale score), and can incorporate nonstandardized achievement score measures such as high school graduation rates or classroom observation data. Using a discrete measure of the level of student performance, as is done under No Child Left Behind, may be viewed as more transparent than using a continuous measure of student performance but is likely to produce inconsistent estimates of teacher performance and may encourage teaching to the bubble. Incorporating nontest score measures may improve the validity and reliability of the system if done well but could just as easily reduce both, depending on which measures are incorporated and how.

The challenge for developing the measure is connected with the aforementioned principles: Don't make it overly complex. At times, program developers may trade an element that might add some more information, but the program also reaches a saturation point of evaluation. Consider that teachers address this same problem in their own classrooms—trying to determine how to measure the performance of their students via tests, quizzes, presentations, and other methods. The measuring process is a balancing act of utility and complexity. To this end, program planners should address questions such as these:

- What measures of student achievement growth will be employed (e.g., existing state standardized exams, national norm-referenced exams, exams used solely for program purposes, etc.)?

- How exactly will growth, or value added, be measured for the student achievement measures chosen? Will the program employ crude measures of growth based on pre–post differences in scores or more sophisticated value-added growth measures based on statistical regression models?
- How can we incorporate student achievement measures that do not lend themselves well to growth, such as exams that do not have pre-scores (e.g., end-of-course exams)?
- What other measures, if any, of student growth might be employed (e.g., attendance rate, disciplinary incidences, graduation rate, etc.)?

Ratings and Rewards

Once the measures of performance have been chosen, program designers must decide how to use that information to reward teachers. Awards can be given to individual teachers, teams of teachers, or all the teachers in the school. These awards can be of the all-or-nothing variety, where teachers either reach their goal or not and earn the fixed award or not. Or teachers might be eligible to receive a variety of different award levels, based on the extent to which they meet their performance goals. Programs can be designed with a fixed sum of award money to be divided among a fixed number of the top-performing teachers. Alternatively, programs can employ award schemes such that all teachers are eligible based on the extent to which they reach their own performance goals, regardless of the number of their peers also earning awards. Finally, program developers can vary the extent to which these goals distinguish among the faculty, either offering a large number of small awards or a smaller number of more substantial awards.

Of course, certain implications follow each of these choices. School-level awards for performance may encourage teacher cooperation but may also result in some teachers not exerting as much effort as they should (the free-rider problem), compared with a system with teacher-level awards. Discrete rewards may serve to increase the visibility of the systems compared with more continuous systems but may also result in low incentive levels for teachers who believe they are far from the discrete cut point used to determine who gets awards. Absolute benchmarks may encourage teacher collaboration and give teachers a sense of a clear goal but may be difficult to justify on technical grounds and may also result in low standards being chosen, as is common in other professions. Rewards that are too small may be ignored by teachers. At the same time, however, rewards that are too large may reduce interest in teaching if potential teachers become concerned about there being too much uncertainty about their future income or too much focus on earnings as opposed to more intrinsic motivators for teacher performance. Specifically, program planners should address questions such as these:

- Will differential awards be offered to individual teachers, or will identical awards be given to all teachers in a group or a full school? Or will the program employ a hybrid model that includes both individual-level effectiveness and schoolwide achievement in each teacher's rating?
- Will awards be continuous based on the extent to which preidentified goals are met, or will rewards be of the all-or-nothing variety?
- If the program offers individual-level awards, to what extent will the awards vary between the best and poorest performers?
- Will the rating system involve any non-student-based measures of teacher effectiveness, such as subjective evaluation from an administrator or a classroom-observation-based measure of instructional strategies?
- Will the awards be different for participants in different categories (e.g., core, non-core, support staff, school administrators)?
- What will the award amounts be for participants in each category?

This laundry list of questions highlights the fact that there is no single merit pay "plan" and the decisions made in each of these categories have real implications for other decisions and for the potential of the program. Program planners must find a balance among multiple priorities and make wise decisions in the face of difficult trade-offs. For example, if program planners choose to value transparency as a primary principle above all others, this will limit the use of sophisticated value-added models to measure student learning growth. Along those lines, a program focused on core subjects as a key priority (which offered greater rewards for core teachers) may face some challenges in the area of collaboration among all school faculty. Similarly, incorporating teacher input into the system may help encourage teacher support for the system and may increase the degree to which the system incentivizes them to exert effort. However, if the resulting system does not identify and reward the best teachers, or properly discriminate between the most effective and least effective teachers, the program may not have its intended effect.

Indeed, there are an infinite number of ways school leaders could implement a merit pay scheme for the educators in their school or district. In the chapter that follows, we take these decision points and place them along a timeline of implementation. Chapter 7 then illustrates an exemplar (and fictional) merit pay program based on our experiences.

6

Timelines for Program Development and Implementation

In the previous chapter, we proposed a set of foundational principles for any merit pay plan and then outlined the many questions that plan developers must consider and answer as part of plan development. After the foundation has been built, school leaders will need to follow a systematic plan to work with program stakeholders to answer the pesky questions we highlighted. The principles and questions described in the prior chapter will be far more helpful, we believe, when provided along with a set of concrete action steps that school leaders could follow during plan development and implementation.

In this chapter, then, based on our experience in developing, implementing, and evaluating these plans, we provide a step-by-step plan and timeline for school leaders interested in implementing merit pay. Our focus in this chapter is on the process of bringing in stakeholders and developing a plan that will be "owned" by all program participants. A plan developed in this way stands the best chance—we believe—of weathering the inevitable opposition and creating the opportunity for successful implementation of a program that may lead to improved student learning in the long term. Additionally, since this chapter is intended to be a "how-to" timeline, we opted to write it to a school administrator directly, so the chapter is written such that the "you" is a principal or administrator currently considering or developing a program.

PROGRAM IMPLEMENTATION TIMELINE

This section is organized as a timeline geared toward a program that will go into effect in the fall of Academic Year 2. Thus, fall of Academic Year 0 is 2 years before the program will go into effect. We believe that a 2-year cycle of planning allows you and program developers enough time to appropriately address the guiding principles and pesky questions discussed in the previous chapter. With that, the remainder of this chapter is dedicated to walking through how to go from "Merit Pay?" to a fully developed and implemented plan.

Step 1: Mulling It Over (Fall Year 0)

If you're reading this book and giving serious consideration to this idea, you have already begun Step 1 by starting to research this reform idea. In our example here, we presume you have begun thinking about implementing this reform strategy in the fall or winter of an upcoming academic year. In this stage, which is at least 18 to 24 months before any program will be implemented, it is worthwhile to read about schools where merit pay programs have been implemented and consider a few key questions.

First, you should consider the source of the *initial funding* for the program. It is likely that, at least early on, the funding for a merit pay program will not be pulled from existing salary funds. Teachers are skeptical enough about this idea that they are not likely to buy in to a program that requires them to risk any of their existing salary! However, in many districts there may well be untapped funds within existing budgets or opportunities for reallocation of existing resources. Moreover, there are numerous opportunities for state and federal grants to support merit pay reform plans (more on this in Chapter 8). Finally, there are also private philanthropic foundations that have shown an interest in supporting programs to offer teacher bonuses based on effectiveness.

As a ballpark to consider how much funding you may need to begin, think about the following brief back-of-the-envelope calculations. If we assume an average teacher salary of $40,000 and a maximum bonus level of 15%, we would need an available $6,000 per teacher. If we assume a school with 30 kids per classroom (elementary school), the maximum cost would be about $200 per student. If we assume 50 teachers in the school, the maximum payout would be $300,000. Understanding that every teacher earning the maximum bonus is certainly ideal but also highly unlikely allows you to budget $300,000 for the bonuses and then carry forward the balance each year.

Second, you should consider the possible reaction of teachers and other stakeholders in the school or district to merit pay. In some settings, particularly in which there is an atmosphere of distrust and opposition between yourself and the teaching faculty, this type of plan would be received poorly, generate nothing but opposition, and inevitably fail. On the other hand, in other settings where the culture may be more accepting of innovation and diverse ideas, you may well be able to navigate around the cautious feelings stakeholders may initially hold toward the idea of merit pay for teachers. In any event, you should informally "take the temperature" of the culture to assess whether the educators might ever warm up to a merit pay proposal.

At this point, if you have decided there may be funding available to support such a program and educational stakeholders would be willing to discuss the idea and not reject it outright, you should move on to the next step.

Step 2: Organizing a Merit Pay Exploratory Committee (Spring Year 0)

As the academic year comes to a close in spring of the given year (more than 15 months before the commencement of the first program year), you should identify potential candidates for a merit pay planning committee. Indeed, in some settings, it may be better to refer to this as an "exploratory" committee to make it clear that no decisions have been made and this controversial idea is simply being considered. In our view, this committee should not be all encompassing; it should be small and manageable and include representatives of all groups that might be influenced by a merit pay plan. A planning committee should include yourself (whichever role you perform in the school) and the following people:

- The district superintendent (or school principal if only a single-school plan)
- Principals from potentially participating schools
- Lead teachers of core subjects
- Lead teachers of non-core subjects
- A representative of school support staff (e.g., school secretary, custodian, etc.)
- A parent representative
- An outside facilitator (researcher or consultant with experience on merit pay in schools)

The composition of this group is important. These members must be open to this idea and able to elicit the concerns of the school community and bring them back to the committee so the product developed by the committee will be appealing to the relevant stakeholders. Committee members will need the wisdom to sort among the genuine fears voiced by dedicated but dubious educators and the complaints of the vocal minority of cantankerous teachers who may not want such a plan.

These committee members must be trusted members of the school, as their role in communicating the details and progress of the plan will be invaluable. For such an idea to gain acceptance, stakeholders must be continually, fully, and accurately informed. It is the duty of this committee to keep the lines of communication wide open (remember Principle 2 from Chapter 5). Finally, members of this committee must have time and energy to dedicate to the task, as this is no small endeavor.

You may have noticed that we also included a researcher or outside consultant to serve as an outside facilitator. There are many questions and issues associated with the consideration and development of a plan that are not obvious. Someone with experience in this area can help the committee anticipate challenges and provide outside perspective on possible responses to the challenges faced. There is no need for each local committee to reinvent the wheel. Further, this person can also serve as an "outsider" who may ask questions and see issues from a different perspective than those within the school or district. Remember, the members of the committee are charged with conceptualizing the plan and discussing it with their respective groups and associates, so the value of the committee is not well served if it is only a select group of people with whom there will be no real discussion. Those who you believe may be the most opposed to the idea may also be potentially good committee members because they will have an opportunity to be part of the conversation and determine if and how a program could be useful within the school.

Step 3: First Meeting With the Exploratory Committee (Summer Year 0 to Fall Year 1)

The first meeting with the committee is critically important in setting the stage for effective planning and productive discussions. In our view, the meeting should be well organized and concise while also allowing input from stakeholders. This is a delicate balance. Even the formal invitation to serve on the committee is important. The main catalyst of the idea (likely you, as the school leader) must develop a letter briefly describing the purpose of the committee while simultaneously underscoring the importance of the task and the fact that this plan is not being dropped on educators from above.

You must be clear from the start that this is an exploratory committee, that no decisions have been made, and that this will be a group-based decision. If not, the second that teachers in the school get wind of a committee meeting about merit pay, there will be rumors that *all future pay raises will be based on proficiency rates on the end-of-course exams.*

One way to ensure that the initial meeting is properly viewed as exploratory is to structure the meeting around a presentation given by an outside expert/researcher/consultant and explicitly geared toward describing the pluses and minuses of merit pay in schools. This presentation should be based on the experiences of educators in other schools where merit pay reform was implemented. By adopting this strategy, you are not taking a stance on one side or the other of this controversial topic. Instead, the topic is brought to a representative team of school stakeholders who can decide as a team whether this is an idea worth pursuing.

Of course, if you have determined that merit pay is going to be implemented, then the function of the committee is to determine how to make it work rather than if it should be tried. However, the committee might decide with unanimous certainty that introducing merit pay would be a disaster. In that case, you would likely have to question the notion of implementing a plan in a resistant environment. However, if a representative committee of educators came out so strongly against merit pay even after a balanced introduction to the topic was presented, then merit pay would likely have failed. Although, this early committee rejection of merit pay would save you from many headaches in the long run! In short, the committee of school representatives is a strong first gauge in determining how well the plan will be received and how effective it will be overall. Remember, even the best-laid plans rarely work without the support of others.

In preparation for the initial meeting with the exploratory committee, it would be worthwhile for you to develop a tentative set of central tenets, or key principles, that should guide the development of the merit pay plan. The objective here is to have something concrete to drive the conversation; otherwise, an unguided discussion focused on a controversial topic such as merit pay has the potential to spiral quickly into negativity. Of course, these central tenets should be flexible so that the planning committee has genuine input and true ownership of the plan from Day 1.

An example of key principles that might be used as a starting point for the proposed Rewarding Achievement With Merit Pay (RAMP) program in a hypothetical school is displayed in the box below. The principles described for the hypothetical RAMP program are general and broad; it will take many hours of work to transform these guidelines into a concrete plan. Nevertheless, the list can provide a starting point for discussion with an exploratory committee that may have little knowledge of merit pay or little interest in pursuing merit pay as a reform strategy.

Trinity Public Schools Exploratory Committee Rewarding Achievement With Merit Pay (RAMP) Five Key Principles

- *Nonpunitive*—Participation in RAMP is voluntary, and there is no risk to base salaries.
- *Focused on student growth*—RAMP teacher ratings are based in part on student growth rather than on point-in-time achievement levels.
- *Encourage collegiality*—RAMP will reward teachers for working together and will not pit teachers against one another for a fixed pot of available awards.
- *Transparent and understandable*—RAMP ratings will be based on a straightforward formula that will be clearly defined at the beginning of the school year.
- *Significant financial rewards*—Educators participating in RAMP will be stepping out of their comfort zone; in return for this, educators will have the opportunity to earn bonuses in the neighborhood of $10,000 per year.

In summary, the first meeting should include a balanced introduction to this topic (perhaps from the outside facilitator) and discussion of the underlying principles that should guide the committee in the consideration and possible development of a plan. As this first meeting adjourns, members of the committee should begin discussions with their colleagues to gauge the level of interest in the possibility of a merit pay plan within the school or district. Early in the next academic year (fall of Academic Year 1), you should reconvene this committee to make a decision as to whether the group actively pushes forward on the development of a plan.

Step 4: Introducing the Concept to the Full School Community (Early Fall Year 1)

Assuming that the planning committee decides the hypothetical RAMP plan has the potential to create positive change in the schools, the committee should quickly introduce the general idea to the full faculty, well before the specific details of the program are considered. At this full faculty meeting, the school leader should introduce the exploratory committee to the faculty and should make very clear that the work is in an exploratory phase. During this meeting, a couple of committee members (including the outside facilitator) should give a presentation on the concept of merit pay that includes the following topic areas.

Sample Introductory Meeting Agenda Items

- Provide a general description of merit pay.
- Discuss why this is being tried in schools today and what positive benefits it might have.
- List some of the places where this strategy is being undertaken.
- Acknowledge the criticisms and discussions of how to avoid common problems (see Chapter 4).
- Highlight some general guidelines that plans should follow (addressed earlier in this chapter).
- Present the central principles identified by the planning committee (or merit pay exploratory committee).
- Describe how such a proposal would be funded.
- Open the floor up to discussion to assess whether this idea is worth exploring further.

The outside facilitator should play a major role here, as faculty members are likely to have many questions that this expert will be best positioned to address. However, it is equally important that local committee members play a role in this presentation to make clear that this is not an idea being foisted on the school community from outside.

It is also important that thoughtful and comprehensive written materials be distributed at this meeting. These materials must present all the key information in a user-friendly format (i.e., this should not read like a boring memo or, worse, like instructions for installing a washing machine). Many faculty will not be at this meeting, and other faculty may not remember all the details presented. And as we noted above under the topic of communication, it is critically important that good information be shared in a timely manner. In the case of missing information, misinformation can quickly fill the gaps, particularly when the issue is controversial. Moreover, transparency and information sharing will go a long way toward building trust among all stakeholders.

Another way to make this initial meeting as useful as possible would be to distribute a presurvey and then a postsurvey to gain some insight into the group's openness to the idea before and after the presentation (see Appendix A for a sample survey). Such a survey could also prove valuable by highlighting any areas where miscommunication has occurred. Appendix A was developed and used in the Achievement Challenge Pilot Project. Appendix B is also provided as an example of an instrument that might be used, and it was developed for the Project on Incentives in Teaching (POINT) project (Springer, Ballou et al., 2010). The postsurvey might be best administered online so that faculty can have some time to reflect on the idea before responding. To enhance the likelihood that faculty will respond to the postsurvey, each respondent should be entered in a random lottery for the chance to win gift cards (or something similar) after successfully completing the survey. This level of detail will also continue to reinforce that this program is from the faculty at the school rather than from outside parties.

In the week or so following, the committee members will circulate among the faculty to gather the level of support or opposition for a merit pay plan. Depending on the size of the faculty, committee members may want to hold a formal vote of the potential program participants before deciding whether to move forward. The committee must be intentional about seeking the feedback of all faculty; while some of the more vocal will always be able to make their opinions known, it is important that the committee also gain insight into the views of the less assertive teachers in the school.

Step 5: Details, Details, Details (Late Fall Year 1)

Assuming the exploratory committee receives the go-ahead from the full faculty to move forward on this idea, the group must then "ramp" up the effort to create a concrete plan that can be shared with the full faculty and other stakeholders. There is a variety of strategies that the committee might employ to flesh out all the important details. In our view, the full committee is well suited to come to a consensus on the guiding principles of the plan but not well suited to develop all the plan's details. Rather, the details of the rating and reward system should be fleshed out by smaller "working groups," who build the system around the generally agreed-on principles. Indeed, most of the specific decisions will be made by the working groups rather than by the exploratory committee. A sample list of working groups could include those shown in the example below.

Trinity Public Schools Exploratory Committee Rewarding Achievement With Merit Pay (RAMP) Working Groups

Elementary and Middle School Math
Elementary and Middle School Literacy
Elementary and Middle School—other tested subjects?
Elementary and Middle School—nontested subjects
High School Math
High School Literacy
High School—other tested subjects?
High School—nontested subjects
School Support Staff
School Administrators
Fundraising or Sustainability Group

The reason for this division of labor is clear—particular members of the exploratory committee would have only the specific knowledge required for certain areas. For example, the high school art teacher would likely have little to add to the discussion of how best to evaluate the effectiveness of middle school teachers of core subjects. Working group members for this area would need to know, for example, the details of the standardized assessments administered to middle school students in core subject areas. Conversely, the middle school math teacher would likely have little useful input on how to properly rate the effectiveness of the high school art teacher.

The outside facilitator would likely have a role in facilitating the work of each of these small working groups. These working groups would spend their time and energy answering the types of questions raised in the prior chapter and getting into all the details, such as how academic growth is measured, what teams should be used for team-based goals, or which exam should be used to measure student learning growth in algebra. The outside researcher can provide some perspective about the types of decisions made in other schools or districts on many issues the working groups face.

The exploratory committee would then decide whether to accept the proposed systems developed by the working groups (concrete examples of a plan will be provided in the chapter that follows).

Step 6: Finalizing and Ratifying the Plan, or "Rocking the Vote" (Spring Year 1)

By the start of the spring semester of Academic Year 1, each of the working groups should have completed its work and should bring the proposed plan details to the full merit pay exploratory committee. Within 4 to 6 weeks, the full committee should agree to a full plan and begin work on sharing this information with the full faculty. At this full faculty meeting, you should remind the faculty of the process that has occurred to this point, introduce the members of each working group, and then begin a 30- to 60-minute presentation of the plan's details.

In this case, you (or even the outside facilitator) should make very clear to the faculty that there is no "one" right outcome for the many decisions that the committee had to make. Instead, the committee members simply did their best to develop detailed rating and reward systems that are as consistent as possible with your program's foundational principles. Moreover, this plan should be viewed as a "living" document that should be tweaked and modified each year after committee members discover some plan aspects that work well and others that need adjustment, which is valuable for the working groups to consider whether they would like to see any changes.

As was the case with the initial full faculty meeting, the outside facilitator should play a major role to answer technical questions. At the same time, local committee members must continue to take on a visible role to continue to make clear that the program is a locally developed plan. Moreover, the committee should distribute comprehensive and reader-friendly written materials to the full faculty; because there will be faculty absent and because faculty will want to refer to these details later, the "draft" plan should also be posted prominently on the school's website.

If any clear objections are voiced during the meeting or if adjustments need to be made before moving the plan from "draft" status to "final" status, the exploratory committee can make changes after this meeting.

Then, after the meeting has occurred and the final version of the plan has been posted on the school's website, the full faculty should be given a week or so to consider the idea and approach exploratory committee members with any follow-up questions. After this step, all that remains is the formal vote of the full faculty. While smaller schools might be able to conduct an in-person vote, larger schools may employ an online vote. The committee must decide which voting mechanism is likely to lead to the greatest participation and to provide the best opportunity for faculty members to feel comfortable in honestly representing their own views.

At this point, if more than three fourths of the faculty support the proposed plan, the exploratory committee should graduate to, for example, a "pay-for-performance" committee, or PfP committee. (For some reason, the term *merit pay* seems to elicit a much more negative reaction than does the term *pay for performance*, but use your own discretion for what works in your school.)

Step 7: Getting Ready to Roll Out the Plan (Summer Year 1 to Fall Year 2)

This is the time when any last minute details must be handled for the program's initial year. Most important, you and the planning committee must decide on how the ratings will be calculated and how the bonuses will be paid out to the school faculty.

Calculation of Ratings and Bonuses

You and the PfP committee must decide whether to do the rating computations or bonus calculations "in-house" or to contract with an outside firm to do this work. The obvious benefit of doing the work within the school or district is that the data are already there and no additional funds are needed to pay the outside contractor. On the other hand, doing this work in-house places an additional burden on school staff that may not have the capacity to undertake this. Further, school officials have noted that the bonus calculations may be viewed as more objective or legitimate if computed by outside "experts." Local school officials will know best which choice is appropriate here.

No matter who is chosen to do the work, planning work in this area should begin in the summer, as the teacher "report cards" should be developed and ready for the faculty when they walk through the school doors in the fall. These report cards should clearly highlight each of the areas where the teachers will be rated and should make the rating scheme transparent to program participants (see Appendix B for a sample report card).

Planning work should also begin during the summer to set the table for the evaluation of program effectiveness. In this case, it is important that an external evaluator be identified who will work to ensure that the necessary pre-data related to the teachers and students are gathered on time.

Payment of Bonuses

This is most certainly a local decision, as issues such as employee fringe rates and tax rates come into play. In some instances, the school office itself pays out the bonuses. In this case, generally, standard benefit fringe rates and tax rates apply so that, for example, a teacher who earns a $10,000 bonus might receive a bonus check that is more in the neighborhood of $7,000. Alternatively, in school districts served by nonprofit public education foundations, the bonus program could be funded and administered by this entity, and then the bonuses may not be subject to the standard benefit rates.

Step 8: Start Your Engines (Fall Year 2)

Relax—you made it! At least you made it to the point where you can start doing the real work—kind of like graduating and then realizing you have to actually perform. Year 0 was tinkering around with an idea; Year 1 represented the planning year, and Year 2 represents the first year of program operation.

As teachers enter the school buildings for the first year in which performance bonuses will be distributed, you and the PfP committee must be prepared to communicate early and often and make sure the lines of communication are wide open. Very early on, teachers should be handed their individual report cards, which articulate the areas where the teacher will be rated and, most important, the students for whom each teacher will be held accountable. In this way, teachers can quickly identify if there are any problems with the student lists or any misunderstandings regarding the operation of the plan.

This is also a good time for you and the PfP committee to develop and administer a brief survey that tracks the perceptions of the program participants regarding merit pay. Ideally, at this point, the faculty will reveal an openness to this idea and perhaps cautious optimism about merit pay. It is important that this type of information be tracked over time.

Step 9: Checking In (Spring Year 2)

During the spring semester of the initial program year, you and the PfP committee should continue to facilitate open lines of communication with faculty by holding an open meeting so faculty may ask any questions or present any problems. For any faculty whose ratings involve the meeting of subjective goals, this is a good time for school administrators to check in with the faculty on their progress with respect to these goals. Of course, many standardized assessments involved in the rating scheme will be administered to students across the school or district during this term as well.

Step 10: Show Me the Money
(Summer Year 2 to Fall Year 3 and Beyond)

In the summer, after the subjective ratings have been made by administrators, the necessary rubrics have been completed, and the standardized test results have been entered, rating calculations can be made (either in-house or by an outside organization).

After the rating calculations are made, the reward amounts are computed, and all the data are double-checked, it is time to distribute the checks to the faculty. It is very important, particularly for the first payout, that the checks are distributed on time and as promised. We must not forget that teachers have some reason to believe that educational fads come and go and that some programs do not come off as promised. Add to this that teachers are already quite skeptical about the idea of merit pay bonuses—and because they involve money, their concerns are legitimate. To be clear, this step is where many merit pay systems fall apart. Don't be among them— plan, plan, and then plan again. Meeting deadlines and being accurate is critically important and will go a long way toward earning the trust of program participants.

At the same time, the PfP committee should hold meetings and focus groups with faculty to assess what worked and what did not work with the program during its first year in operation. This is also a good time to conduct a post-survey of the teachers regarding their views on the fairness of merit pay plans in general and of this plan in particular. As the committee evaluates the concerns of teachers, the group must be willing to discriminate between reasonable concerns and silly ones. That is, the PfP committee should not make changes to the plan based on every concern raised. Most important, the committee should be willing to reevaluate the plan from year to year. This requires a balance whereby the plan's foundational principles remain intact, but the details should be flexible (e.g., what percentage of the award relies on team goals vs. individual goals, which tests are employed, etc.). When changes are made, the committee must continue to pay great attention to communication and make clear to program participants that any small changes are made for the purpose of improving the plan and not for finding a way to undermine rewards to teachers.

In this chapter, we have set forth a proposed timeline (which is, of course, flexible) that might be used as a guideline for a school leadership team considering, developing, and implementing a merit pay plan for educators in the district. In the chapter that follows, we will present an example plan that might evolve from this process. The plan we describe is flexible but is also based on the key principles we highlighted in Chapter 5. This is the type of plan, we believe, that has a strong chance of leading to positive changes for students and teachers in your school or district.

7

RAMP

*Ramping Up Teacher Pay in
Your School*

In the previous chapters, we proposed a set of foundational principles, outlined a set of critical questions, and proposed a detailed timeline for program
development and implementation. All that is left now is to sketch out the framework of a merit pay plan that can serve as an exemplary program from which to
begin such conversations. This chapter serves that purpose. To begin laying out
an exemplary proposed program, we first review some of the key understand-
ings we gained through our experiences and the literature on merit pay.

The Achievement Challenge Pilot Project (ACPP) was the first merit
pay program we worked with, nearly a decade ago. This program had several positive characteristics—teacher bonuses were based on the extent to
which their own students made gains in achievement throughout the year,
the bonuses were substantial, all school staff were program participants, and
there was no "zero-sum" aspect that caused only a set number of participants to earn an award. However, there were certainly still potential areas
for improvement. For example, classroom teachers' bonuses were based on
student performance on a single exam and were not based at all on schoolwide achievement. Moreover, this plan was developed from the outside and
did not include any intentional attempt to garner teacher buy-in.

On the other hand, the Denver ProComp plan was developed based on a collaboration of numerous stakeholder groups and employs an exhaustive (and highly
complicated) formula for computing teacher ratings and bonuses (see Figure 7.1).

Figure 7.1 2010-2011 ProComp Payment Opportunities

Component of Index $37,551	Knowledge and Skills			Comprehensive Professional Evaluation			Market Incentives		Student Growth			
Element	Professional Development Unit	Advanced Degree and License	Tuition and Student Loan Reimbursement	Probationary	Non-Probationary	Innovation Non-Probationary	Hard-to-Serve School	Hard-to-Staff Assignment	Student Growth Objectives	Exceeds CSAP Expectations	Top Performing Schools	High Growth School
Description of Element	Providing ongoing professional development–is tied to the needs of our students–is a central strategy to help you expand your skills, improve student performance, and advance your career with the district	Compensation for graduate degree or advanced licenses or certificates	Reimbursement for tuition or for outstanding student loans	Increases for new teachers based on a satisfactory evaluation	Increases based on a satisfactory evaluation	Increases based on a satisfactory evaluation	Designed to attract teachers to schools with a high free and reduced lunch percentage	Designed to attract teachers to roles with high vacancy rate and high turnover	Incentive paid for meeting student growth objectives	Teachers whose assigned students' growth in CSAP scores exceeds district expectations	Teachers in schools designated as a "Top Performing School" based on the DPS School Performance Framework	Teachers in schools designated as a "High Growth School" on the DPS School Performance Framework
Eligibility and Payout	Base building for PDUs paid if 14 or fewer years of service. Non-base building if more than 14 years of service at time of payment	Paid upon receipt of documentation that the license or certification is active and current	Paid upon receipt of evidence of payment for and satisfactory completion of coursework; $4,000 lifetime account; no more than $1,000 per year	Requires satisfactory evaluation; if unsatisfactory, ineligible for CPE increase	Payable only to teachers who have a formal evaluation during service credit years 1 through 14	Teachers receive 1% of index increase for a satisfactory annual evaluation during years 1 through 14 if have not received a 3% of index CPE increase in the past 2 years	Teachers currently serving in schools designated "hard to serve"	Teachers currently serving in designated "hard to staff" positions	Base building when 2 SGOs are met, non-base building when only 1 SGO is met during prior school year[4]	Paid based on assigned student CSAP growth percentiles; paid based on results from prior school year	Paid based on performance during the prior school year	Paid based on performance during the prior school year

Effect on Base Salary	Base building[2]	Base building	Non-base building	Base building	Base building	Base building	Non-base building	Non-base building	Base building[4]	Non-base building	Non-base building	Non-base building
Percentage of Index	2%	9% per degree or license; eligible once every 3 years	N/A	1% every year	3% every 3 years	1% every year if no 3% in past 2 years	6.4%	6.4%	1%	6.4%	6.4%	6.4%
Dollar Amount	$751	$3,380	Actual expense up to $1,000/ year, $4,000 lifetime	$376	$1,127	$376	$2,403 $200.27/ month	$2,403 ($200.27/ month) x (# of assignments held)	$376.00	$2,403.26	$2,403.26	$2,403.26
Builds Pension and Highest Average Salary	Yes	Yes	No[3]	Yes	Yes	Yes	Yes	Yes	Yes	Yes	Yes	Yes
Payment Type and Frequency[6]	Monthly installments upon submission of proper documents	Monthly installments upon submission of proper documents	Up to $1,000 per year upon submission of proper documents	Prorated over 12 months; if unsatisfactory, delayed at least 1 year	Prorated over 12 months; if unsatisfactory, delayed at least 1 year	Prorated over 12 months; if unsatisfactory, delayed at least 1 year	Monthly installment upon completion of service each month	Monthly installment upon completion of service each month	One objective: paid lump sum. Two objectives: paid in monthly installments	Paid lump sum in the year following assessment	Paid lump sum in the year following assessment	Paid lump sum in the year following assessment

Source: Denver Public Schools (http://denverprocomp.dpsk12.org/). Used with permission.

Important Notes:

–These amounts and terms are based on the agreement approved by DCTA membership. ProComp pay referenced in this document is based on an index amount of $37,551. Amounts are based on 1 FTE (except for Tuition Reimbursement) and are prorated.

–Top Performing Schools and High Growth Schools incentives are based on the School Performance Framework, which you can read about on the Denver Public Schools website. The exact targets for determining the schools receiving these incentives are set by the Transition Team.

–ProComp participants who will have 14 or fewer years of service credit during the contract year in which the PDU is paid will receive a salary increase of 2% of the salary index for the contract year in which the PDU is paid.

–ProComp participants who will have more than 14 years of service credit during the contract year in which the PDU is paid will receive a non-salary–building bonus of 2% of the payment year's salary index.

1. Builds base salary for teachers with 1 to 14 years of service credit and does not build base salary for teachers with 15 or more years of service credit.

2. Builds base salary for teachers with 1 to 14 years of service credit and does not build base salary for teachers with 15 or more years of service credit.

3. All incentives except Tuition Reimbursement are pensionable. In other words, all ProComp payments are taken into account in calculating your highest salary on which your pension is based.

4. Regarding the Student Growth Objectives, teachers will receive the payout in a non-base-building lump sum if one objective is met, and as a base-building payment if two objectives are met.

5. Service Credit - The years of full-time contract experience recognized by DPS, which may include experience outside the Denver Public Schools. Years of service is different from Longevity. Longevity includes service at DPS only.

6. See ProComp MoU Payment matrix for more detail on timing of payments.

While there are obvious strengths implicit in ProComp's collaborative development and use of multiple measures of teacher effectiveness, this program necessarily is less transparent to participants and results in a lesser focus on student achievement.

We might have also chosen to highlight the Nashville Project on Incentives in Teaching (POINT; see Springer, Ballou et al., 2010), although this merit pay experiment is noteworthy more for the random assignment design of its evaluation than for the design of the alternative compensation structure. A key strength of this merit pay plan was the magnitude of the bonuses (up to $15,000 per effective teacher) and the clear focus on student achievement growth. However, like the ACPP plan, this plan suffers from its sole focus on the effectiveness of individual teachers based on student achievement. Thus, if there were to be benefits from a team of educators pursuing a shared goal, such benefits would not be observed in this plan. Furthermore, because the significant awards were bestowed only on the top teachers among all teacher participants, it is possible that many participants did not view the awards as attainable. Thus, the fact that POINT did not result in measurable student gains should not necessarily be viewed as damning to the potential benefits of a well-structured merit pay plan.

Finally, the New York City merit pay plan studied by RAND (Fryer, 2011) was built quite differently than the POINT plan. The rewards were group based, given to all faculty in schools that met certain achievement levels. A strength of this program is that it was focused on economically disadvantaged schools and thus aimed to encourage great teachers to work with poor students. Nevertheless, due to the reasonably small award level ($3,000 per teacher) and the schoolwide-only nature of the award, it would not be surprising if individual teachers did not feel particularly motivated to alter their behavior, given the small influence that their own individual effort would have on schoolwide achievement.

Each of these four programs exemplified some positive program characteristics along with some limitations. In our hypothetical exemplar plan, examined in the following pages, we attempt to capitalize on the strong points of other programs while making alterations where needed to address the limitations. As a result, to provide an illustration of how we believe a merit pay program can work, we have constructed a fictional program in a fictional school district. In creating this program and district, we rely on our extensive experience working in a variety of states and districts, including urban, suburban, rural, and tribal districts.

We considered presenting detailed examples of several program schemes (such as the four touched on earlier) so the reader would have the opportunity to consider multiple program design options. However, we decided that a better use of the finite pages in this chapter would be to present a detailed outline of a single plan based on what we have learned in working with and observing numerous design options. In other words, we did not want to spend time and space describing a plan in detail and then discussing why we don't think such a plan will work! Instead, we present here a broad outline of a plan that we believe can be successful; the plan we present allows for a great deal of flexibility so that school leaders can adapt it to meet the needs and preferences of the local community.

As noted during the key considerations and principles chapters, we absolutely believe that a program must be tailored to a local community and that it must be supported by the local educators. We believe our hypothetical RAMP (Rewarding Achievement With Merit Pay) program in the hypothetical Trinity Public School District can provide a strong example of how to design and implement a program with the greatest chance of success. The RAMP program revolves around the guiding principles we presented in Chapter 5. While we refer to the RAMP program as fictional, it may be even more accurate to view RAMP as an amalgam of the numerous plans we have developed in recent years in collaboration with educators in traditional public schools and charter schools from Arizona to Arkansas and Colorado to New York.

RAMP: APPLYING THE PRINCIPLES

First of all, following the guiding principles, the RAMP plan is designed to be as clear and understandable as possible for the participants. The ratings are based on a 100-point scheme, which is transparent and should be familiar to educators. To make this rating scheme clear, merit rating "report cards" will be distributed to all participants at the beginning of each school year to illustrate the level of achievement expected of his or her students and to show exactly how the year-end bonus will be calculated (see Appendix C).

Second, the RAMP ratings will be based on multiple measures of teacher effectiveness. As noted earlier, teachers have many objectives to meet. While the task of fostering student learning is likely the most important goal pursued by most teachers, it is not the only aim we expect teachers to pursue. Along those lines, the RAMP rating is based both on student learning gains and the subjective evaluation of supervisors. Moreover, one of the great challenges facing designers of merit pay plans is evaluating the effectiveness of non-core teachers, such as teachers of fine arts or physical education. Since it is difficult to directly assess the impact of non-core teachers on student learning, plan designers must consider alternative measures of effectiveness for these teachers (remember from Chapter 6 that this information can be developed in the working groups).

Third, the RAMP plan will rate participants based on the extent to which they reach their 100-point goal and will allocate rewards based on that rating. We believe this strategy is superior to one in which only the top set of teachers are rewarded; such "zero-sum" schemes can certainly discourage collegiality. Indeed, the RAMP plan will encourage collegiality by basing the rating for each participant both on individual teacher effectiveness and overall school performance. Thus, each participant's rating will actually benefit from the good work of his or her peers, which improves overall school performance. In this way, the RAMP program will encourage collaboration and collegiality among program participants, who will all be awarded as they pursue the common goal of schoolwide student achievement.

Furthermore, the RAMP plan will encourage collegiality by including all school employees as participants. While different types of school employees have different levels of impact on student achievement, we maintain that each employee does play a role and an optimal merit pay plan should include all employees. However, it is also true that some employees (e.g., teachers of core, tested subjects) bear a greater responsibility and face greater pressure to improve student achievement. Thus, the RAMP plan will rate and reward all school employees, but different types of school employees will be eligible for different maximum bonus levels.

Speaking of bonus levels, and consistent with our guiding principles, the RAMP program will offer substantial and meaningful bonuses (otherwise, why go through the effort of designing and implementing a plan?). Participants in the RAMP plan will be eligible for annual bonuses of up to $10,000 if they reach their performance goals. Funding for the hypothetical RAMP program was provided by a Teacher Incentive Fund (TIF) grant from the U.S. Institute of Education Sciences. As we mentioned earlier, there are several pathways to funding a program—federal or state grants, private foundations, and/or shifting around existing budgets or bonus accounts. For RAMP, the program is a 5-year grant, where the funding decreases each year by 20% as the federal dollars are frontloaded to cover the initial costs, and then the district begins to take on the costs. For Year 1 of the RAMP program, the TIF covers 100% of the payouts; for Year 2, the TIF covers 80%, with the district covering 20%; for Year 3, the TIF covers 60%, with the district picking up 40%; for Year 4, the TIF covers 20% and the district covers 80%; and, finally, in Year 5, the TIF covers 0% and the district covers 100%. In this way, the district is increasingly responsible for the program, and the TIF money is allocated to cover the front end of the program.

While it is not necessary for the operation of a merit pay plan, we propose that such a reform may have a better chance of being useful if employed as part of a comprehensive school improvement strategy, or at least alongside another complementary reform. As we noted in Chapter 5, the implementation of a formative assessment system that assesses student performance at multiple points throughout the school year would fit well with our proposed plan. Such an assessment system, such as the MAP system built and provided by the Northwest Evaluation Association (NWEA), allows teachers to engage in continuous performance monitoring to track student progress regularly and systematically. Moreover, such a system of computer-adaptive testing of student achievement is one of the more accurate ways to track annual gains in learning for groups of students and can be very useful in the evaluation of effectiveness of individual teachers.

A few other characteristics of the RAMP program distinguish this program from other merit pay programs. The most noteworthy of these is RAMP's smooth award structure that does not include unnecessary "cliffs" in the award structure stemming from dichotomous rating schemes. That is, the RAMP program does not offer a fixed award for those who meet their goals, as did the New York City Merit Pay Program, which awarded $3,000 per teacher in schools that met goals and $0 to teachers in schools that did not. In such a structure, very small changes in overall performance (such as one that moves a teacher or school from just above to just below the cutoff point) can lead to large changes in awards. Particularly in regard to a task such as measuring student learning, in which our estimates are imperfect, we do not prefer such dichotomous rating strategies that crudely categorize teachers as either meritorious or not.

Instead, the aptly titled, fictional RAMP program's award structure can be thought of as an actual ramp, whereby participants earn additional awards as their performance ramps up to the 100-point performance goal. For example, if a teacher earned 80/100 points, or 80% of the total possible points, then the teacher would earn 80% of the maximum bonus amount. If this teacher were a core teacher eligible for the maximum bonus of $10,000, he or she would receive a year-end performance pay bonus of $8,000. In this example, if that teacher had earned 79 instead of 80 points, he or she would receive an award of $7,900 instead of $8,000. The key point here is that, in the RAMP plan, small changes in measured performance and teacher ratings lead to correspondingly small changes in merit awards.

We base these program characteristics on the research highlighting problems in past merit pay plans, the criticisms levied by opponents of merit pay plans, and our own experience in numerous schools in a variety of contexts. When taken together, these factors should not only lead to a positive school climate and culture among teachers and staff but also to marked improvements in levels of student achievement. The following section provides an overview of the hypothetical RAMP performance pay plan in the hypothetical Trinity Public School District. Again, recall that we created this fictional program based on an amalgamation of our experiences of working with districts and schools, and it is intended as a guide that avoids the common pitfalls we have experienced while maximizing the greatest anticipated benefits.

RAMP: GENERAL OVERVIEW

In the hypothetical RAMP bonus plan, every Trinity Public Schools employee is eligible for a performance-pay bonus. The maximum bonus for which each employee is eligible will vary for various types of employees. Similarly, the components of the supervisor evaluation and the teacher-specific effectiveness will be different for different types of teachers. This bonus is based on the total number of points an employee earns on a 100-point scale, which contains different criteria (most of which are directly tied to student achievement) depending on the job classification of the employee. Figure 7.2 represents the general criteria used to determine the merit ratings and accompanying performance-pay bonuses for teachers within the RAMP plan.

Figure 7.2 Option 1: Distribution of Points in RAMP Rating Model

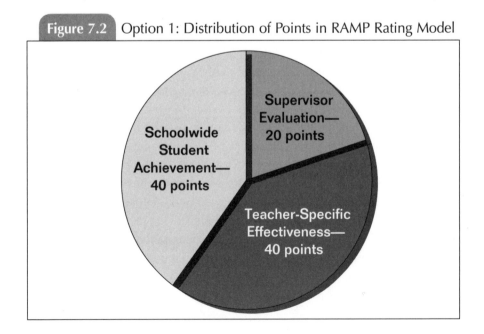

The general model is based on the guiding principles discussed above. First of all, the 100-point plan is a format that should be understandable and familiar to most in the business of education. By basing a meaningful portion of the award (20%) on supervisor evaluation, the RAMP plan acknowledges that multiple measures are meaningful. Furthermore, by basing the rating both on individual teacher effectiveness and overall school performance, the RAMP plan explicitly builds in a focus on collaboration. Furthermore, because participants are rated based on the extent to which they reach their 100-point goals, there is no reason for participants to sabotage the ratings of their peers.

At this point, we want to make very clear that there is no magic formula in these numbers, no precision attached to our recommendations. In this example, we propose a rating scheme that evenly weights individual effectiveness and overall group performance because both are important. However, these are just suggestions; depending on the local context, it might be just as reasonable for a school to choose a 60/30/10 split among individual performance, schoolwide achievement, and subjective evaluation. Decisions regarding the weighting of these categories should be made by the school leaders and/or the planning team. We are not arguing that one particular weighting scheme is better than another, but we do believe it is appropriate to include each of these three categories in the rating system.

Thus, in this section, we are presenting a set of guidelines along with a discussion of the options available within those guidelines. Based on this structure, a potentially successful program can be designed. While we have thus far presented a general overview of the RAMP plan, we have conveniently omitted important details on how each of these sections will be rated. In the section that follows, we will delve into these details, moving from the least complex to the most.

RAMP: DETAILS

Supervisor Evaluation (20 Points)

Teachers and other school employees perform several roles that are not directly connected to student achievement. Some teachers are more likely than others to volunteer for committee assignments, to take a new teacher under their wing, or to go out of the way to mentor students. Similarly, some school staff are more collegial, punctual, and professional than their peers. These practices or behaviors can influence how smoothly a school runs on a daily basis and are thus reflective of a school employee's contribution to the overall school culture. In this section, such teacher behaviors, both positive and negative, can be captured in the teacher's overall merit rating.

In the RAMP program, we have allotted 20 points for this category; this may work well in schools or districts in which there is a great deal of trust between the faculty and administrators. In other schools or districts, in which teachers may fear that favoritism could sneak into subjective evaluations by administrators, a lower weight could be placed on this category.

In our experience, these supervisor evaluations are based on rubrics completed by principals, assistant principals, or other direct supervisors. Presumably, the principal would evaluate the classroom teachers, the superintendent would evaluate the principals, and perhaps an assistant principal might evaluate the custodian or the school receptionist.

Schoolwide Student Achievement (40 Points)

Throughout this book, we have discussed the importance of collegiality and creating a merit pay plan that rewards all school employees for working toward the school's common goal of improving student achievement. In the RAMP plan, we have chosen to weight schoolwide achievement equally with individual effectiveness, and this deserves some discussion.

There is a strong argument to be made for using schoolwide, or group-based, ratings of educational effectiveness. According to proponents of this view, the education endeavor does not lend itself well to the evaluation of individual contributions to student learning. As some educators might say, learning is a complex, co-produced outcome in which the learner and many teachers play a role. A student's achievement in math, for example, might be influenced by his current math teacher, as well as his math teacher from the prior year, his science teacher from the current year, and his own initiative. Thus, it may be easier to accurately account for the contributions to student learning made by a team of teachers than to isolate the contribution of a single teacher. Lazear (2003) and others have further noted that group incentives can serve to foster feelings of fairness and group unity. Finally, in the field of education, where the mere mention of the term *merit pay* can lead to concern over the divisive competition that is sure to follow, programs may well have a better chance for success if they include a team-based component.

However, there is also an argument to be made for individual ratings, as the use of group team incentives does not come without its share of limitations. Foremost among these is the well-known free-rider problem, whereby individuals within teams may choose to exert minimal effort, understanding that they can "free-ride" off the efforts of their teammates. Thus, all else equal, individuals have lower levels of motivation than if consequences were attached to their individual behaviors. This problem is not insurmountable; in smaller teams, peer pressure can serve to encourage individual efforts among team members and offset the free-rider problem.

Compelling reasons support the use of both individual-based incentives and team-based incentives. Thus, many schools and districts are opting to employ a hybrid model in which the incentive structure incorporates the unique contribution of individual teachers while also employing group-based rewards to foster collaboration and teamwork among teachers. Practically, the hybrid plans may be viewed favorably by teachers, as they are rewarded for the achievement of their own individual students and for the achievement of students of all other teachers in the team. This scheme reduces the likelihood that teachers will avoid collaboration with their peers or, worse, seek to sabotage the performance of students in the classrooms of peer teachers—a drastic outcome, but this problem might emerge in small ways or even more egregious ways. At the same time, because hybrid plans also incorporate the performance of a teacher's individual classroom students, the free-rider concern can be mitigated.

For all these reasons, we prefer this "hybrid"-rating type of program and have recommended it to the districts with whom we have partnered. We recommend it here as we suggest an even split (40/40) between individual-teacher and team goals.

In practice, there is a variety of ways to evaluate group-based performance or schoolwide performance. These include the following:

- Improvements on state standardized exams in mathematics
- Improvements on state standardized exams in English/language arts
- Extent to which all students in schools meet annual growth goals on standardized formative assessment in mathematics
- Extent to which all students in schools meet annual growth goals on standardized formative assessment in language
- Improvements in student performance on other measures such as ACT, SAT, or AP exams
- Non-standardized-achievement-test–based measures such as schoolwide attendance rate, graduation rate, incidence of disciplinary infractions, or other similar measures related to overall student well-being

How to allocate the 40 points for schoolwide performance among the categories above is, in our opinion, a local decision. For elementary schools and middle schools, the focus may be on the state exams or formative assessments, since most students in the school will be assessed annually. For high schools, on the other hand, it may be appropriate to include other measures such as graduation rate or student performance on college entrance exams such as the ACT or SAT.

Moreover, school leaders could also incorporate the achievement of particular subgroups of students in the category of schoolwide performance.

For example, in a school experiencing particular trouble working with its lowest performing students, school leaders might want to make this a point of emphasis and reward the staff for addressing this problem. The merit pay plan would be one place where school leaders could signal the importance of the issue by, for instance, splitting up the 40 points for schoolwide performance in the following way:

- 10 points—improvement on state standardized exams in mathematics
- 10 points—improvements on state standardized exams in English/language arts
- 10 points—improvement on state standardized exams in mathematics *for the lowest performing quartile of students in the school*
- 10 points—improvements on state standardized exams in English/language arts *for the lowest performing quartile of students in the school*

Just as there is no right or wrong way to allocate the 100 points to the three key categories, there is also no single correct strategy for divvying up these 40 points. The appropriate division varies based on the age of the students in the school, the availability of data, and the needs of the local school or district at the time. Indeed, school leaders would likely choose to modify these categories from time to time as new areas of need emerge in the school or district. Remember, the purpose of the plan is to encourage faculty and staff to work toward certain goals (see Figure 7.3 for another example).

Figure 7.3 Option 2: Distribution of Points in an Evaluation Model

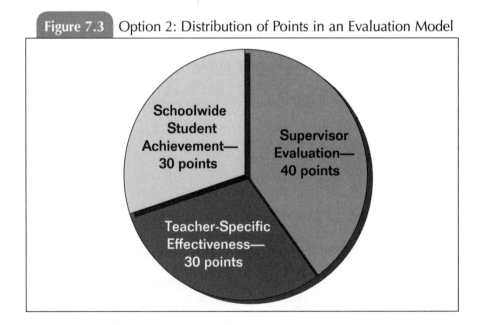

In the case of the RAMP example program, we choose a reasonably simple allocation and set it up for middle school grades (in this way, we are considering a set of grades likely to include state standardized exams) in a school that has adopted a formative testing system (e.g., NWEA's MAP program).

Individual Classroom Achievement (40 Points)

This category is the most complicated and requires the most explanation because the computation methods must vary for the type of employee. Thus, before we describe our ideas on rating individual effectiveness, we must first discuss the different types of school employees. Obviously, schools have many types of employees, and we could create numerous categories if we chose; however, our general strategy is to organize the program as simply as possible. Thus, we propose the creation of three categories of school employees. First, we refer to those teachers who teach core subjects that include some sort of regular assessment as "core teachers." Core teachers include those responsible for teaching core subjects such as reading, mathematics, science, and social studies. Second, we refer to the remaining educators in the school as "non-core teachers." Counselors, band teachers, art teachers, and physical education teachers are examples of non-core teachers. Finally, we refer to other school staff as "school support staff." Examples of support staff include custodians, school receptionists, bus drivers, and school lunch staff. The measures of individual effectiveness will, of course, vary based on the category of the staff member.

Core Teachers

The work of these teachers is particularly amenable to evaluation based on quantifiable measures of growth in student achievement. It is reasonable to suggest that the primary responsibility of core teachers is to foster student learning in these foundational subjects. For teachers of mathematics and English/language arts, the work they do is tied directly to assessments annually administered to students. Thus, it seems quite reasonable to evaluate a middle school math teacher, for example, based on the growth of his or her students on standardized assessments of mathematics knowledge.

There are two general types of exams described above that we might use: (1) annually administered state standardized exams and (2) computer-adaptive assessments administered at multiple times throughout the school year. There are reasons to prefer each of these. The state exams are presumably well aligned with the state's curricular standards, which represent what students are to be learning in school each year. However, these exams generally do not have the psychometric properties that make them well suited to measures of student growth, and they are administered only once per year. On the other hand, computer-adaptive assessments, such as the afore-mentioned NWEA MAP, are suited for measuring student growth (based on each student's pretest at the start of the school year, an expected score for each student at the year-end can be derived). However, these exams may not be perfectly aligned with state curricular standards (this weakness may be ameliorated in the future if more states adopt a common set of standards).

Nevertheless, because each exam provides valuable information but is imperfect on its own, we suggest that, for core teachers, the 40 points dedicated to individual teaching effectiveness be based equally on student improvement on state exams in the relevant subject area (20 points) and on student growth on the computer-adaptive formative assessment in that same subject area (20 points).

In many instances, deciding what tests to use will not be as easy as described above. What about social studies or science teachers? It is certainly true that most states do not have standardized tests in each of these areas; thus, school leaders will have to be creative when deciding how to evaluate such teachers. There are a few options. First, such teachers could be treated as non-core teachers, as we will describe in the next section. Alternatively, school leaders could identify outside assessments that effectively measure student learning in social studies or science. Finally, we have worked with schools where the ratings for social studies teachers are based on student growth on language arts exams and the ratings for science teachers are based on student growth on math exams. To repeat an important theme—there is no single right answer here other than that the solution must be locally determined.

Non-Core Teachers

Historically, the work of non-core teachers has been less amenable to standardized evaluation based on quantifiable measures of growth in student achievement. (Holheide, Browder, Warren, Buzick, & Jones, 2012) Recognizing the value of all teachers in education, many states and districts have continued to investigate how all teachers can be evaluated effectively, including the use of Student Learning Objectives (SLOs) for non-standardized subjects. (e.g. Browder, Wakeman, Ahlgrim-Delzell, & Hudson, 2011; Jun, Gomez, Baird, & Keramidas, 2008; Lohmeier, 2009; Morta, 2010) We have previously worked in school districts where non-core teachers (e.g., physical education teachers, art teachers, band instructors) have been evaluated nearly entirely based on schoolwide student achievement (as described above). This strategy appeared to cause consternation among these teachers, as they viewed themselves as having very little direct control over the vast majority of their merit rating. In meetings with faculty, many non-core teachers indicated that such a rating strategy ignored nearly all of what these teachers were expected and professionally obligated to do for their students. While it is true that all teachers contribute to a culture of success and achievement, it is also true that much of what teachers do (particularly non-core teachers) is not reflected in math and reading scores.

As the evidence and experience base on evaluating non-core teachers continues to emerge, we encourage merit pay program developers to continue investigating how other states and districts are using SLOs. As an example of how an SLO might be developed, we recommend that the 40 points associated with individual teaching effectiveness be based on individual goals identified (and mutually agreed on) at the beginning of each year during a meeting between the principal (or relevant assistant principal) and the teacher. Some examples of professional goals for non-core teachers include the following:

- For a *physical education*—teacher who is also a coach—this teacher will be evaluated on the extent to which he or she increases the participation rate on the team (10 points), the success of the team (10 points), the attendance rate of players throughout the school year (10 points), and the grade point average of players throughout the school year (10 points).
- For a *band instructor*—this teacher will be evaluated on the extent to which he or she increases the number of students participating in band (10 points), the success of the band in external band competitions (10 points), the attendance rate of band members throughout the school year (10 points), and the grade point average of band members throughout the school year (10 points).
- For an *art teacher*—this teacher will be evaluated on the extent to which he or she incorporates lessons that will improve student reading and writing (20 points) and the success of the art students in external art competitions (20 points).

In keeping with a recurring theme, there is no right or wrong way to engage in this subjective evaluation style, except that the goals must be identified and made clear to the non-core teachers at the *beginning* of the school year.

While the process of developing these goals in principal–teacher meetings at the beginning of each year can be time-consuming, it can also encourage useful conversations in which school leaders and faculty discuss individual goals and the schoolwide mission. Another potential weakness of this strategy is that it may well involve subjectivity; however, principals are most certainly professionals, and it seems reasonable to allow for some subjectivity and discretion, particularly in areas where there are not better, more objective strategies available. Several states and districts continue to refine their approach for using SLOs and provide extensive information on their process for creating and measuring them. One pioneering effort in developing these measures is the Austin Independent School District (see http://archive.austinisd.org/inside/initiatives/compensation/slos.phtml).

School Support Staff

The individual work of school support staff is similar to that of non-core teachers in that it is not amenable to evaluation based on quantifiable measures of growth in student achievement. As we do in the case of non-core teachers, we recommend that the 40 points associated with school support staff be based on individual goals identified (and mutually agreed on) at the beginning of each year during a meeting between the staff member and his or her supervisor. Some examples of professional goals for support staff include the following:

- For a *custodian*—this staff member will be evaluated on the extent to which he or she improves on the response time to messes in the school (10 points) and on the rating of the general cleanliness of the school based on weekly observations by the supervisor (30 points).
- For a *school receptionist*—this staff member will be evaluated on the extent to which he or she improves on the friendliness and timeliness exhibited in interacting with students, staff, and guests at the school (20 points) and on his or her ability to take on some additional recordkeeping tasks assigned by the principal (10 points).

Administrators

The inclusion or exclusion of the administration in a program is the same as all the other decisions. The individual work of an administrator can certainly impact the school environment, the core and non-core teachers, and the support staff. However, the difficulty is in the details of measuring change. New measures are being created and implemented to gauge how principals and administrators are impacting the school. The Vanderbilt Assessment of Leadership in Education (VAL-ED) is one such instrument. The VAL-ED is based on six core components and six key processes, which create a matrix of 36 elements (see Figure 7.4).

Within the RAMP program, we would use growth in the VAL-ED scores from year to year as 50 points and schoolwide student achievement growth as 50 points. To this end, the 50 points from the VAL-ED might also be based without the involvement of the principal's self-assessment so as to reduce any perverse incentive for evaluating oneself.

Summary

This RAMP outline is meant to serve as a framework and the details as suggested strategies for addressing the numerous questions that must be answered in the process of developing a plan. The purpose of the working groups is to detail exactly how the points will be awarded and how they will translate into dollars. There is not one best way to set up these parameters, and all these decisions should be made based on the unique situation in the participating school or district. The only requirement is that the parameters

Figure 7.4 Vanderbilt Assessment of Leadership in Education

	Key Processes					
Core Components	Planning	Implementing	Supporting	Advocating	Communicating	Monitoring
High standards for student learning						
Rigorous curriculum (content)						
Quality instruction (pedagogy)						
Culture of learning and professional behavior						
Connections to external communities						
Performance accountability						

Source: Porter, A.C., Polikoff, M.S., Goldring, E.B., Murphy, J., Elliott, S., & May, H. (2011). Investigating the validity and reliability of the Vanderbilt Assessment of Leadership in Education. Figure 2 "VAL-ED Conceptual Framework." *Elementary School Journal, 111*(2).

be set and communicated before the beginning of each school year. In fact, it is best if school faculty and staff are involved in the process of setting up some of the details so all participants buy in to the program.

Translating the Ratings Into Dollars

Thus far, we have discussed how the 100-point merit score is computed for various types of school faculty and staff, but we have not yet discussed dollars and cents. This is deliberate; the ratings are distinct from the maximum possible awards for each employee category. The big question facing school leaders here is whether and how much to differentiate the award levels between the different types of employees.

In most districts in which we have worked, school leaders have suggested different levels of reward eligibility for core teachers, non-core teachers, and support staff. The logic behind this is that teachers with the greatest responsibility for improving student learning in the core subjects have the greatest responsibility overall and face the greatest pressure, and thus should be in line for the greatest potential awards. Non-core teachers, who also have direct teaching responsibility, but in non-core areas, should be eligible for substantial awards but not at the level of core teachers. Finally, support staff are eligible for the lowest level of awards because they are the furthest away from the students in the classroom; however, they are still important contributors to the overall school culture and, as such, should be part of the RAMP program.

We are not going to suggest that there is an exact set of reward levels that is the "correct" one to incentivize and award teachers appropriately. Obviously, local issues such as the availability of funding will strongly influence the award levels employed in any merit pay program. Nevertheless, we are willing to offer a recommendation. Thus, in the hypothetical RAMP program described here, core teachers will be eligible for a maximum award level of $10,000, non-core teachers for $8,000, school support staff for up to $2,000, and administrators for up to $5,000.

Then the final computation of the year-end bonus for each teacher is straightforward. For each faculty and staff member, regardless of category, the total number of "merit" points earned (80 points, for example) is then divided by 100, which results in the percentage of the maximum bonus the RAMP participant will receive. In the case of a core teacher who earned 80% of the possible merit points, this teacher would earn 80% of the maximum bonus amount. Since core teachers, in this example, are eligible for a maximum bonus of $10,000, this teacher would receive a year-end merit pay bonus of $8,000.

CLOSING

Throughout this chapter, we have articulated a hypothetical sample program and described the decisions necessary at each stage. We have provided a thorough "workshop"-style presentation of issues, and the resounding statement is that many decisions are made at the local level. As with any other group, for teachers to become part of a program, buy-in is important. For the teachers to buy in, we believe that thoughtful conversations within working groups is important to articulate how different groups might create their payout formulas.

In examining Chapters 5 through 7, we see the connections between the guiding principles, the timeline, and the details of a program. The exploratory committee and the working groups must work together to establish how the program will work in operation, so once the report cards are created, they are reminders of what is important for the school and for each group. The final chapter of this book pulls these concepts together and situates them within the relevant literature discussed previously.

8

Conclusions

We believe the value of this book is in responding to a need by providing a detailed summary of the evidence on merit pay and providing a clear "how-to" guide for developing a plan. Throughout the preceding chapters, we provided a discussion of guiding principles, key questions, an example timeline, and an exemplar program. The remaining two issues for many educators are how to find the resources to support such a program and what they can expect from it.

FINDING FUNDING

As states are continuing to develop myriad plans to reduce costs, the notion of taking on a new compensation structure seems daunting for many. However, with personnel costs accounting for about 70% of most educational budgets, the personnel areas are also already being tapped. In many schools, fewer teachers are being hired, and some teachers are being furloughed. However, the question is, how are we determining who should be released? In many instances, these releases are based on seniority, which follows a certain rationale. Notwithstanding, the most senior teachers may or may not be the most effective teachers. Creating a merit-based plan such as RAMP, where teachers have agreed to the evaluation measures, would seemingly be a much more effective manner of reducing personnel when needed. It would also be an effective way to know when and who to rehire once resources free up again.

Barring the short-term problem with the economy, the costs of a merit pay plan also can largely be absorbed by restructuring the existing payroll plans. That is, consider the bonuses attached to years of experience and additional degrees, which could be reallocated to merit or proportionally reallocated. However, from our perspective, states should cover these additional costs of education. Currently, the federal government is providing resources via the Teacher Incentive Fund and Teacher Quality Partnership grants, as well as through the Race to the Top competition for programs aimed at altering the existing compensation structure and evaluation of teachers (see http://www2.ed.gov/programs/teacherincentive/index.html and http://www2.ed.gov/programs/racetothetop/index.html).

The Race to the Top and Teacher Incentive Fund grant competitions have awarded nearly $6 billion into the educational system of states and districts, much of which has gone directly to educator evaluation and compensation reform. As such, the federal government is able to cover the costs for most of the start-ups (generally 5 years) of the program, which allows time to reallocate resources and get a firm grasp on the cost of the program at your local school. The newly announced district-level Race to the Top competition is also a rich resource for developing an alternative compensation program. Beyond these federal dollars, various state governments have also provided resources toward recruiting and rewarding effective educators, including Minnesota's Q-comp program, Nevada's teacher bonus program, and Texas's District Awards for Teacher Excellence.

Additionally, a number of private organizations are inclined to support efforts to alter the current compensation and evaluation structure to be based on more established criteria aligned to student achievement. These organizations may have direct competitions dedicated to compensation reform, or they may have resources dedicated to education in general, and they may be approached for solicited funds to evaluating, recruiting, and rewarding effective educators. We have worked directly with or know that the following organizations have provided funding for compensation reform programs: the Bill & Melinda Gates Foundation, Carroll and Milton Petrie Foundation, and Kauffman Foundation.

Moreover, while the focus is often on garnering outside funds, we should not overlook the possibility that school leaders can seek ways to reallocate existing funds. For example, in many states, districts serving many low-income students receive categorical funds aimed at improving instruction and achievement for these economically disadvantaged students. In these same districts, school leaders often struggle to find experienced teachers and thus have large numbers of inexperienced, and relatively low-paid, teachers on staff. In many cases, school leaders in these districts use categorical funds or surplus personnel funds to hire additional teachers; school leaders could instead allocate some of these funds into performance bonus programs in an effort to recruit and retain the best teachers.

Similarly, school leaders are often able to find resources to purchase curricular programs or other programs at the cost of several hundred dollars per child. While many of these programs may well be productive, it may also be worthwhile for school leaders to consider allocating roughly $500 per student toward a teacher performance bonus program. Even this relatively small per-pupil allocation could allow the district to implement a significant bonus program for teachers and ultimately for the good of students.

EXPECTATIONS FOR YOUR PROGRAM

The final issue for creating a merit pay program is understanding and articulating expectations for the program. As we noted throughout the earlier chapters, clear communication is vital to the success of creation and implementation of the program; however, a clear understanding of what the program will accomplish is also necessary. Remember that the value of a merit pay program is that it is intended to be both motivational and compositional in effect. That means it can alter the overall attitude of the teachers and staff in the school, who are now working in a much more aligned manner and being rewarded for doing so. And more teachers inclined to work within such an environment will be drawn into your school. To be clear, these changes can take several years to go into effect. Expectations should be measured over time for the impact of the program; however, as with any plan or program, it is unlikely to revolutionize the performance of students in a single year.

CLOSING

The crescendo accompanying merit pay discussions is outside the schoolhouse doors. Policymakers across the country, including at the national, state, and local levels, are looking for systematic ways to change the educational system. As discussed in Chapter 2, merit pay has emerged on the educational landscape due to the foundation afforded by a decades-old accountability movement that is now also complemented by robust technological advancement, where data can be readily collected, stored, and reviewed. The evidence on merit pay will continue to grow as more programs are developed and implemented. As educators continue to sift through the debate on merit pay, we aim to provide a concise and straightforward guide.

You now have all the criteria to begin considering how to create a merit pay program. We encourage you to review the timeline and guiding principles as you begin the process of developing a plan. Go forward with confidence!

Appendix A

Sample Teacher Survey

Appendix A: Sample Teacher Survey

Please indicate your level of agreement with the statements below by checking the appropriate box:

		Strongly Disagree	Disagree Somewhat	Agree Somewhat	Strongly Agree
1	I am satisfied with the current teacher salary system.	1 ☐	2 ☐	3 ☐	4 ☐
2	I think merit-pay programs increase collaboration among teachers.	1 ☐	2 ☐	3 ☐	4 ☐
3	If I have many low-performing students in my class, it is a burden.	1 ☐	2 ☐	3 ☐	4 ☐
4	Teachers at my school get along well with each other.	1 ☐	2 ☐	3 ☐	4 ☐
5	An end-of-year evaluation by the principal is an appropriate measure of my effectiveness.	1 ☐	2 ☐	3 ☐	4 ☐
6	Teachers who have more teaching experience are generally more effective at teaching than those with less experience.	1 ☐	2 ☐	3 ☐	4 ☐
7	Teachers who have advanced degrees are generally more effective at teaching than those without advanced degrees.	1 ☐	2 ☐	3 ☐	4 ☐
8	Gains in student test scores are appropriate measures of teacher effectiveness.	1 ☐	2 ☐	3 ☐	4 ☐
9	If I have many low-performing students in my class, it is an opportunity to demonstrate my teaching ability.	1 ☐	2 ☐	3 ☐	4 ☐
10	I am paid well for the amount of effort that I put into my work.	1 ☐	2 ☐	3 ☐	4 ☐
11	I think pay-for-performance programs lead to counterproductive competition between teachers.	1 ☐	2 ☐	3 ☐	4 ☐
Over the last school year, …		Strongly Disagree	Disagree Somewhat	Agree Somewhat	Strongly Agree
12	I researched more new teaching strategies than in previous years.	1 ☐	2 ☐	3 ☐	4 ☐
13	I collaborated more with other teachers.	1 ☐	2 ☐	3 ☐	4 ☐
14	I have enjoyed teaching in my school.	1 ☐	2 ☐	3 ☐	4 ☐
15	I spent less time working in the evenings on school related work.	1 ☐	2 ☐	3 ☐	4 ☐
16	I worked harder than I've worked in previous years.	1 ☐	2 ☐	3 ☐	4 ☐

Please continue the survey on the back

Over the last school year, …	Strongly Disagree	Disagree Somewhat	Agree Somewhat	Strongly Agree
17 I talked with other teachers about our professional development training.	1 ☐	2 ☐	3 ☐	4 ☐
18 The culture in my school has become more negative.	1 ☐	2 ☐	3 ☐	4 ☐
19 I talked with other teachers in my school about new teaching methods.	1 ☐	2 ☐	3 ☐	4 ☐
20 I talked with other teachers in my school about changing the curriculum.	1 ☐	2 ☐	3 ☐	4 ☐
21 I talked with other teachers about committee, team, or school problems.	1 ☐	2 ☐	3 ☐	4 ☐
22 I talked with other teachers about each others' families, vacations, local sports, or news.	1 ☐	2 ☐	3 ☐	4 ☐
23 I spent more time preparing for my job.	1 ☐	2 ☐	3 ☐	4 ☐
24 I implemented new "best practices" teaching strategies.	1 ☐	2 ☐	3 ☐	4 ☐
25 I withheld ideas about teaching rather than sharing with other teachers.	1 ☐	2 ☐	3 ☐	4 ☐
26 My work environment became more positive.	1 ☐	2 ☐	3 ☐	4 ☐
27 I spent more time preparing for my job.	1 ☐	2 ☐	3 ☐	4 ☐
28 I used the same teaching strategies I used previously.	1 ☐	2 ☐	3 ☐	4 ☐
29 I noticed that other teachers shared fewer of their ideas.	1 ☐	2 ☐	3 ☐	4 ☐
30 Being a teacher has become more difficult.	1 ☐	2 ☐	3 ☐	4 ☐
31 I became a better teacher.	1 ☐	2 ☐	3 ☐	4 ☐
32 Student performance improved in my school.	1 ☐	2 ☐	3 ☐	4 ☐

33. Years of Teaching Experience: _____

34. Highest Degree Completed (example: Master's of Education): _____

35. Grade(s) & Subject(s) Taught: _____

Thank you for completing our survey!

Source: Barnett (2007).

Appendix B

*Project on Incentives in Teaching
(POINT) Teacher Survey*

Category: MNPS standards

- I analyze students' work to identify the MNPS mathematics standards students have or have not yet mastered.
- I design my mathematics lessons to be aligned with specific MNPS academic standards.

[All items answered: Never (1), once or twice a year (2), once or twice a semester (3), once or twice a month (4), once or twice a week (5), or almost daily (6)]

Category: Use of instructional time

- Aligning my mathematics instruction with the MNPS standards.
- Focusing on the mathematics content covered by TCAP.
- Administering mathematics tests or quizzes.
- Reteaching topics or skills based on students' performance on classroom tests.
- Reviewing test results with students.
- Reviewing student test results with other teachers.

[All items answered: Much less than last year (1), a little less than last year (2), the same as last year (3), a little more than last year (4), or much more than last year (5)]

Category: Practicing test-taking skills

- Increasing instruction targeted to state or district standards that are known to be assessed by the TCAP.
- Having students answer items similar to those on the TCAP (e.g., released items from prior TCAP administrations).
- Using other TCAP-specific preparation materials.

[All items answered: No importance (1), low importance (2), moderate importance (3), or high importance (4)]

Category: Time devoted to particular teaching methods in mathematics

---

- Math students spending more time on:
- Engaging in hands-on learning activities (*e.g.*, working with manipulative aids).
- Working in groups.

[All items answered: Much less than last year (1), a little less than last year (2), the same as last year (3), a little more than last year (4), or much more than last year (5)]

Category: Time outside regular school hours

- During a typical week, approximately how many hours do you devote to school-work outside of formal school hours (e.g., in the evenings, before the school day, and on weekends)?

Category: Level of instructional focus

- I focus more effort on students who are not quite proficient in mathematics, but close.
- I focus more effort on students who are far below proficient in mathematics.

[All items answered: Never or almost never (1), occasionally (2), frequently (3), or always or almost always (4)]

Category: Use of test scores

- Use test scores for the following purposes:
- Identify individual students who need remedial assistance.
- Set learning goals for individual students.
- Tailor instruction to individual students' needs.
- Develop recommendations for tutoring or other educational service for students.
- Assign or reassign students to groups.
- Identify and correct gaps in the curriculum for all students.

[All items answered: Not used in this way (1), used minimally (2), used moderately (3), or used extensively (4)]

Category: Collaborative activities with other mathematics teachers

- Analyzed student work with other teachers at my school.
- Met with other teachers at my school to discuss instructional planning.
- Observed lesson taught by another teacher at my school.
- Had my lessons observed by another teacher at my school.
- Acted as a coach or mentor to other teachers or staff in my school.
- Received coaching or mentoring from another teacher at my school or from a district math specialist.

[All items answered: Never (1), once or twice a year (2), once or twice a semester (3), once or twice a month (4), once or twice a week (5), or almost daily (6)]

Source: National Center for Performance Incentives. Used with permission.

Appendix C

Sample Report Card

Bonus Calculation Sheet: Core Teachers

G

Teacher Name: _____

School Name: _____

Job Title: _____

Subject(s) Taught: _____

I. Supervisor Evaluation: 10 Points

a. Adheres to School Policies _____

b. Content Knowledge _____

c. Level of Instruction _____

d. Interacts with Others Professionally _____

e. Professional responsibilities _____

f. **Total Points Earned (a + b + c + d + e)** [ ]

Supervisor Evaluation— 20 points

Schoolwide Student Achievement— 40 points

Teacher-Specific Effectiveness— 40 points

Maximum Payout: **$10,000**

II. Schoolwide Achievement Growth: 40 Points (10 possible pts. for each category)

a. Statewide Math Test Growth _____   d. NWEA Eng/Lang. Growth Goal Met _____

b. Statewide Literacy Test Growth _____

c. NWEA Math Growth Goal Met _____   e. **Total Points Earned (a + b + c + d)** [ ]

III. Teacher-Specific Effectiveness: 40 Points (20 possible pts. for each category)

a. Teacher-Specific State Test Growth _____

b. Teacher Specific NWEA Growth _____

c. **Total Points Earned (a + b)** [ ]

Calculation of Year-End Bonus

a. Supervisor Evaluation _____   d. Total Points (A + B + C) _____

b. Schoolwide Achievement Growth _____ e. **Total Bonus Earned (D/100) x $10,000** [$]

c. Teacher -Specific Effectiveness _____

Bonus Calculation Description Sheet:

Core Teachers

<u>Areas of Evaluation & Total Points Possible:</u>

I) Supervisor Evaluation - 20 pts.

The supervisor evaluation is based on the supervisor's assessment of the teacher in five areas:

- Adheres to School Policies (2 pts.) – Does the teacher adhere to policies and exhibit professionalism, perform responsibilities in a prompt and efficient manner, and participate in school activities?
- Content Knowledge (2 pts.) – Does the teacher seek opportunities to grow professionally, demonstrate advanced knowledge in subject area and utilize test data in planning, and exceed state required professional development hours to enhance teaching practices?
- Level of Instruction (2 pts.) – Does the teacher display evidence of teacher preparation/planning, incorporate higher-level thinking skills and a variety of instructional strategies, and manage all activities and behaviors effectively?
- Interactions with Others (2 pts.) – Does the teacher meet weekly to collaborate with staff members, enhance parental involvement, and implement suggestions from administration and colleagues to improve classroom management and instruction?
- Professional Responsibilities (2 pts.) – Does the teacher adequately meet his or her responsibilities as appropriate to the role of a professional educator?

A teacher is evaluated in each area by his or her principal, with a maximum of 2 points for each area of the evaluation. Points earned in each area are then added, resulting in the total amount of points earned in this category. (**Note: A teacher must earn at least 5 points in the Supervisor Evaluation section for those points to count toward the year-end bonus.** For example, if a teacher only earned 4 out of 10 points, then those 4 points would not be used in the calculation of the bonus.)

II) Schoolwide Growth - 40 pts.

Schoolwide State Math Exam Growth is calculated by adding the number of students that test at the proficient level or advanced level on the statewide math assessment. After adding those two groups of tests together, that total is divided by the number of valid tests, resulting in a percentage of tests showing proficient or advanced level. This percentage is then multiplied by 10 points, resulting in the total amount of points earned in this category.

Schoolwide State Literacy Exam Growth is calculated by adding the number of students that test at the proficient level or advanced level on the statewide literacy assessment. After adding those two groups of tests together, that total is divided by the number of valid tests, resulting in a percentage of tests showing proficient or advanced level. This percentage is then multiplied by 10 points, resulting in the total amount of points earned in this category.

Schoolwide NWEA Math Growth Goal is calculated by subtracting the schoolwide average on the NWEA math pre-test from the schoolwide average on the NWEA math post-test, which results in the average schoolwide NWEA growth. The average schoolwide NWEA growth is then divided by the target growth (target growth is based on a nationwide sample of students who take the NWEA exam each year), resulting in a percentage of target growth achieved. This percentage is multiplied by 10 points, resulting in the total amount of points earned for schoolwide NWEA growth.

Schoolwide NWEA English/Language Arts Growth Goal is calculated by subtracting the schoolwide average on the NWEA English/Language Arts pre-test from the schoolwide average on the NWEA English/Language Arts post-test, which results in the average schoolwide NWEA growth. The average schoolwide NWEA growth is then divided by the target growth (target growth is based on a nationwide sample of students who take the NWEA exam each year), resulting in a percentage of target growth achieved. This percentage is multiplied by 10 points, resulting in the total amount of points earned for schoolwide NWEA growth.

IV) Teacher-Specific Effectiveness - 40 pts.

Individual Teacher/Subject-Specific Exam Growth is calculated by adding the number of students that test at the proficient level or advanced level on the statewide assessment used to evaluate individual teacher performance. After adding those two groups of tests together, that total is divided by the number of valid tests, resulting in a percentage of tests showing proficient or advanced level. This percentage is then multiplied by 20 points, resulting in the total amount of points earned in this category.

Individual Teacher/Subject-Specific NWEA Growth Goal Individual classroom NWEA growth is calculated by subtracting the classroom average on the NWEA pre-test from the classroom average on the NWEA post-test, which results in the average classroom NWEA growth. The average classroom NWEA growth is then divided by the target growth (target growth is based on a nationwide sample of students who take the NWEA exam each year), resulting in a percentage of target growth achieved. This percentage is multiplied by 20 points, resulting in the total amount of points earned for individual classroom NWEA growth.

References

All American Patriots. (2007, July 9). *Chris Dodd: Dodd statement for merit pay for teachers* [Web log comment]. Retrieved from http://www.allamericanpatriots .com/48726583_chris_dodd_chris_dodd_dodd_statement_merit_pay_teachers

Amrein-Beardsley, A. (2012). Recruiting expert teachers into high-needs schools: Leadership, money, and colleagues. Education Policy Analysis Archives, 20(27). Retrieved from http://epaa.asu.edu/ojs/article/view/941

Bacolod, M., DiNardo, J., & Jacobson, M. (2009). *Beyond incentives: Do schools use accountability rewards productively?* (NBER Working Paper No. 14775). Cambridge, MA: National Bureau of Economic Research. Retrieved from http://www.nber.org/papers/w14775

Ballou, D. (2001). Pay for performance in public and private schools. *Economics of Education Review, 20,* 51–61.

Barnett, J. H. (2007). *How does merit pay change schools? A review of the research and evaluation of the impacts of the Achievement Challenge Pilot Project.* University of Arkansas Dissertation. AAT 3302648.

Barnett, J. H., & Openshaw, R. (2011). Changing salaries, changing minds: Examining the merits of merit pay. *Journal of Contemporary Issues in Education, 6*(1), 24–34.

Barnett, J. H., Ritter, G. W., Winters, M. A., & Green, J. P. (2007). *Evaluation of year one of the Achievement Challenge Pilot Project in the Little Rock School District.* Fayetteville: Department of Education Reform, University of Arkansas. Retrieved from http://heartland.org/sites/all/modules/custom/heart-land_migration/files/pdfs/20772.pdf

Belfield, C., & Heywood, J. (2007). Performance pay for teachers: Determinants and consequences. *Economics of Education Review, 27,* 243–252.

Berliner, D. C. (2014). Effects of inequality and poverty vs. teachers and schooling on America's youth. *Teachers College Record, 116*(1).

Breglio, V. (2006, November). *Teachers and top students address a career in educa-tion.* Washington, DC: National Center on Education and the Economy for the New Commission on the Skills of the American Workforce. Retrieved from http://www.skillscommission.org/wp-content/uploads/2010/05/NCEE_Report_ Final_Draft.pdf

Browder, D. M., Wakeman, S., Ahlgrim-Delzell, L., & Hudson, M. (2011). *Utilization of formative assessments within educational programs for students with significant cognitive disabilities: Current practice, current research, and next steps.* Washington DC: Council of State School Officers, Assessing Special Education Students, State Collaborative on Assessment and Student Standards.

Cochran-Smith, M., Feiman-Nemser, S., McIntyre, J., & Demers, K. E. (2008). *Handbook of research on teacher education: Enduring questions in changing contexts* (3rd ed.). New York: Routledge.

Cohn, E., & Teel, S. J. (1991). *Participation in a teacher incentive program and student achievement in reading and math.* Columbia: South Carolina University, Columbia College of Business Administration. (ERIC Document Reproduction Service No. ED340709)

Community Training and Assistance Center. (2004, January). *Catalyst for change: Pay for performance in Denver.* Boston: Author.

Darling-Hammond, L. (2006a). Assessing teacher education: The usefulness of multiple measures for assessing program outcomes. *Journal of Teacher Education, 57*(2), 120–138. doi: 10.1177/0022487105283796

Darling-Hammond, L. (2006b). Constructing 21st-century teacher education. *Journal of Teacher Education, 57*(3), 300–314. doi: 10.1177/0022487105285962

Darling-Hammond, L. (2012, March 5). Value-added teacher evaluation. *Education Week.* Retrieved from http://www.edweek.org/ew/articles/2012/03/05/24darlin ghammond_ep.h31.html?tkn=XSLF8dtEku7dtKu1xSZfeIqk1QmVLXJ5Fp0i& cmp=clp-edweek

Darling-Hammond, L., & Sykes, G. (2003). Wanted: A national teacher supply policy for education: The right way to meet the "highly qualified teacher" challenge. *Educational Policy Analysis Archives, 11*(33). Retrieved from http://epaa. asu.edu/epaa/v11n33/

Dee, T., & Keys, B. J. (2004). Does merit pay reward good teachers? Evidence from a randomized experiment. *Journal of Policy Analysis and Management, 23*(3), 471–488.

Dee, T. S., & Keys, B. J. (2005). Dollars and sense: What a Tennessee experiment tells us about merit pay. *Education Next, 5*(1), 60–67.

Dowling, J., Murphy, S. E., & Wang, B. (2007). *The effects of the career ladder program on student achievement.* Phoenix: Arizona Department of Education. Retrieved from http://www.ade.az.gov/asd/careerladder/CareerLadderReport .pdf

Eberts, R., Hollenbeck, K., & Stone, J. (2002). Teacher performance incentives and student outcomes. *Journal of Human Resources, 37*(4), 913–927.

Eckert, J. (2009). More than widgets; TAP: A systematic approach to increased teaching effectiveness. *National Institute for Excellence in Teaching Reports.* Retrieved from http://www.tapsystem.org/resources/resources.taf?page=ffo_ rpts_eckert

Figlio, D. N., & Kenny, L. (2006, October). *Individual teacher incentives and student performance* (Working Paper No. 12627). Cambridge, MA: National Bureau of Economic Research. Retrieved January 2, 2007, from http://papers. nber.org/papers/w12627

Fryer, R. G. (2011). *Teacher incentives and student achievement: Evidence from New York City Public Schools* (NBER Working Paper No. 16850). Cambridge, MA: National Bureau of Economic Research. Retrieved from http://www.nber .org/papers/w16850

Glass, G. (1995, December). *Discussion of the Tennessee value added assessment system* [Web log comment]. Retrieved from http://gvglass.info/TVAAS/

Glazerman, S., Chiang, H., Wellington, A., Constantine, J., & Player, D. (2011). *Impacts of performance pay under the Teacher Incentive Fund: Study design report.*

Mathematica Policy Research, Inc. Retrieved from http://www.mathematica-mpr
.com/publications/PDFs/education/performpay_TIF.pdf

Glazerman, S. (2004). *Teacher compensation reform: Promising strategies and feasible methods to rigorously study them* (Report No. 3935). Washington, DC: Mathematica Policy Research.

Glazerman, S., Goldhaber, D., Loeb, S., Raudenbush, S., Staiger, D., & Whitehurst, G. J. (2010, November 17). *Evaluating teachers: The important role of value-added*. Washington, DC: Brookings Institution. Retrieved from http://www .brookings.edu/research/reports/2010/11/17-evaluating-teachers

Glazerman, S., & Seifullah, A. (2010, May 17). *An evaluation of the Teacher Advancement Program (TAP) in Chicago: Year two impact report*. Chicago: Mathematica Policy Research. Retrieved from http://www.mathematica-mpr .com/publications/pdfs/education/tap_yr2_rpt.pdf

Goldhaber, D. (2002). The mystery of good teaching. *Education Next, 1,* 50–55.

Goldhaber, D., & Brewer, D. (1997). *Evaluating the effect of teacher degree level on educational performance*. Washington, DC: National Center for Education Statistics, U.S. Department of Education.

Goldhaber, D., DeArmond, M., Player, D., & Choi, H. J. (2008). Why do so few public school districts use merit pay? *Journal of Education Finance, 33*(3), 262–289.

Goldstein, D. (2011, March 3). *Duncan: Test scores not the best way to evaluate art, music, gym teachers* [Web log comment]. Retrieved from http://www.dana-goldstein.net/dana_goldstein/2011/03/duncan-test-scores-not-the-best-way-to-evaluate-teachers-of-nontraditional-subjects.html

Good, T. L., McCaslin, M., Tsang, H. Y., Zhang, J., Wiley, C. R. H., Bozack, A. R., et al. (2006). How well do 1st-year teachers teach: Does type of preparation make a difference? *Journal of Teacher Education, 57*(4), 410–430. doi: 10.1177/0022487106291566

Goodman, S., & Turner, L. (2010, June 3–4). *Teacher incentive pay and educational outcomes: Evidence from the NYC bonus program*. Paper presented at the Program on Education Policy and Governance Working Papers Series, Harvard Kennedy School. Retrieved from http://www.hks.harvard.edu/pepg/ MeritPayPapers/goodman_turner_10-07.pdf

Handler, J. R., & Carlson, D. L. (1984). *Shaping Tennessee's master teacher program—1983. Part 1: Improving teacher quality through incentives project*. Washington, DC: Department of Education. (ERIC Document Reproduction Service No. ED023369)

Hanushek, E. A. (2003). The failure of input-based resource policies. *Economic Journal, 113*(485), 64–68.

Hanushek, E. A. (2007). The single salary schedule and other issues of teacher pay. *Peabody Journal of Education, 82*(4), 574–586.

Harris, D. N. (2011). *Value-added measures in education: What every educator needs to know*. Cambridge, MA: Harvard Education Press.

Harris, D. N., & Sass, T. R. (2007). *Teacher training, teacher quality and student achievement* (CALDER Working Paper No. 3). Washington, DC: The Urban Institute.

Harvey-Beavis, O. (2003, June 4–5). *Performance-related rewards for teachers: A literature review*. Paper distributed at the Organization for Economic Cooperation and Development "Attracting, Developing and Retaining Effective

Teachers" Conference, Athens, Greece. Retrieved November 22, 2006, from http://www.oecd.org/dataoecd/17/47/34077553.pdf

Hassel, E. A., & Hassel, B. C. (2007). *Improving teaching through pay for contribution.* Washington, DC: National Governors Association. Retrieved from http://www.nga.org/files/live/sites/NGA/files/pdf/0711IMPROVINGTEACHING.PDF

Heck, R. H. (2009). Teacher effectiveness and student achievement: Investigating a multilevel cross-classified model. *Journal of Educational Administration, 47*(2), 227–249.

Holdheide, L., Browder, D., Warren, S., Buzick, H., & Jones, N. (2012). *Summary of using student growth to evaluate educators of students with disabilities: Issues, challenges, and next steps: A forum of state special education and teacher effectiveness experts and researchers.* National Comprehensive Center for Teacher Quality. Retrieved March 4, 2013 from http://www.tqsource.org/pdfs/TQ_Forum_SummaryUsing_Student_Growth.pdf

Horan, C. B., & Lambert, V. (1994). *Evaluation of Utah career ladder programs.* Salt Lake City: Utah State Office of Education. (ERIC Document Reproduction Service No. SP035206)

Is the merit pay debate settled? (2011, July 20). *Hechinger Report.* Retrieved from http://hechingerreport.org/content/is-the-merit-pay-debate-settled_6004/

Issue clash: Merit pay. (2009, April 30). *Now on PBS.* Retrieved from http://www.pbs.org/now/shows/518/merit-pay-debate-print.html

Johns, H. E. (1988). Faculty perceptions of a teacher career ladder program. *Contemporary Education, 59*(4), 198–203.

Jordan, H. R., Mendro, R., & Weerasinghe, D. (1997, July). *Teacher effects on longitudinal student achievement: A preliminary report on research on teacher effectiveness.* Paper presented at the National Evaluation Institute, Indianapolis, IN.

Jun, L. A., Gomez, C., Baird, S. M., & Keramidas, C. G. (2008). Designing intervention plans: Bridging the gap between individualized education programs and implementation. *Teaching Exceptional Children, 41*(1), 26–33.

Kelley, C. (1998, May). The Kentucky school-based performance award program: School-level effects. *Educational Policy, 12,* 305–324.

Kelley, C. (2000). *Douglas County Colorado performance pay plan.* Madison, WI: Consortium for Policy Research in Education.

Ladd, H. F. (1999). The Dallas school accountability and incentive program: An evaluation of its impacts on student outcomes. *Economics of Education Review, 18,* 1–16.

Lazear, E. P. (2003). Teacher incentives. *Swedish Economic Policy Review, 10,* 179–214. Retrieved from http://www.government.se/content/1/c6/09/54/30/5cf67673.pdf

Lohmeier, K. L. (2009). Aligning state standards and the expanded core curriculum: Balancing the impact of No Child Left Behind. *Journal of Visual Impairment and Blindness, 103*(1), 44–47.

Marsh, J. A., Springer, M. G., McCaffrey, D. F., Yuan, K., Epstein, S., Koppich, J., et al. (2011). *A big apple for educators: New York City's experiment with school-wide performance bonuses.* Santa Monica, CA: RAND. Retrieved from http://www.rand.org/content/dam/rand/pubs/monographs/2011/RAND_MG1114.pdf.

McCarty, B. J. (1986). An axiological analysis of the master teacher concept (merit pay) (Doctoral dissertation, Oklahoma State University, 1986). *Dissertation Abstracts International, 47,* 3298.

Morta, A. L. (2010). *A rubric and individualized education plan to increase academic achievement in middle school students with disabilities.* Ann Arbor, MI: ProQuest LLC. (ERIC Document Reproduction Service No. EDS514159).

Murnane, R. J., & Cohen, D. K. (1986). Merit pay and the evaluation problem: Why most merit pay plans fail and a few survive. *Harvard Educational Review, 56,* 1–17.

Odden, A. (2000). New and better forms of teacher compensation are possible. *Phi Delta Kappan, 81,* 361–366.

Odden, A., & Kelley, C. (1997). *Paying teachers for what they know and do: New and smarter compensation strategies to improve schools.* Thousand Oaks, CA: Corwin Press.

Plucker, J. A., Zapf, J. S., & McNabb, S. A. (2005). Rewarding teachers for students' performance: Improving teaching through alternative teacher compensation programs. *Center for Evaluation & Education Policy: Education Policy Brief, 3*(5).

Podgursky, M. J. (2002). *The single salary schedule for teachers in K–12 public schools.* Discussion paper prepared for the Center for Reform of School Systems, University of Missouri–Columbia. Retrieved from http://web.missouri.edu/~podgurskym/papers_presentations/reports/teacher_salary_schedules.pdf

Podgursky, M. (2007). Teams versus bureaucracies: Personnel policy, wage-setting, and teacher quality in traditional public, charter, and private schools. In M. Berends, M. G. Springer, & H. Walberg (Eds.), *Charter school outcomes.* Mahwah, NJ: Lawrence Erlbaum.

Podgursky, M. J., & Springer, M. G. (2007). Teacher performance pay: A review. *Journal of Policy Analysis and Management, 26*(4), 909–950. doi: 10.1002/pam.20292

Ritter, G. W., & Holley, M. (2008, March 17). Time for testing. *Arkansas Democrat-Gazette.*

Rivkin, S. G., Hanushek, E. A., & Kain, J. F. (2005). Teachers, schools, and academic achievement. *Econometrica, 73*(2), 417–458.

Rothstein, R., Ladd, H. F., Ravitch, D., Baker, E. L., Barton, P. E., Darling-Hammond, L., et al. (2010). *Problems with the use of student test scores to evaluate teachers* (Economic Policy Institute Briefing Paper No. 278). Washington, DC: Economic Policy Institute. Retrieved from http://www.epi.org/publication/bp278/

Rowan, B. (2002). *What large-scale, survey research tells us about teacher effects on student achievement: Insights from the prospects study of elementary schools.* Ann Arbor: University of Michigan.

The Royal Commission on the state of popular education in England. (1861). *Parliamentary Papers, 21.*

Sanders, W., & Rivers, J. (1996, November). *Cumulative and residual effects of teachers on future student academic achievement.* Knoxville: University of Tennessee Value-Added Research and Assessment Center.

Scherer, M. (2001, May). Improving the quality of the teaching force: A conversation with David C. Berliner. *Educational Leadership, 58*(8), 6–10.

Shulman, L. S. (1988). A union of insufficiencies: Strategies for teacher assessment in a period of educational reform. *Educational Leadership, 46*(3), 36–41.

Silman, T., & Glazerman, S. (2009). *Teacher bonuses for extra work: A profile of Missouri's career ladder program.* Princeton, NJ: Mathematica Policy Research.

Springer, M., Ballou, D., Hamilton, L., Le, V., Lockwood, J., McCaffrey, D., et al. (2010). *Teacher pay for performance: Experimental evidence from the Project on Incentives in Teaching.* Nashville, TN: National Center on Performance Initiatives.

Springer, M., Ballou, D., & Peng, A. (2008). *Impact of the Teacher Advancement Program on student test score gains: Findings from an independent appraisal.* Nashville, TN: National Center on Performance Initiatives.

Springer, M., Lewis, J., Ehlert, M., Podgursky, M., Crader, G., Taylor, L., et al. (2010). *District Awards for Teacher Excellence (D.A.T.E.) Program: Final evaluation report.* Retrieved from http://www.performanceincentives.org/data/files/news/BooksNews/FINAL_DATE_REPORT_FOR_NCPI_SITE.pdf

Springer, M., Lewis, J., Podgursky, M., Ehlert, M., Gronberg, T., Hamilton, L., et al. (2009, August 31). *Texas Educator Excellence Grant (TEEG) Program: Year three evaluation report.* Nashville, TN: National Center on Performance Incentives. Retrieved from https://my.vanderbilt.edu/performanceincentives/files/2012/10/200908_SpringerEtAl_TEEG_Year31.pdf

Springer, M., Lewis, J., Podgursky, M., Ehlert, M., Taylor, L., Lopez, O., et al. (2009, July 27). *Governor's Educator Excellence Grant (GEEG) Program: Year three evaluation report.* Nashville, TN: National Center on Performance Incentives. Retrieved from https://my.vanderbilt.edu/performanceincentives/files/2012/10/200907_SpringerEtAl_GEEG_Year2.pdf

Springer, M., & Winters, M. (2009). *New York City's school-wide bonus pay program: Early evidence from a randomized trial.* Nashville, TN: National Center on Performance Initiatives.

Strauss, V. (2010, September 29). Ravitch: The long, failed history of merit pay and how the Ed Department ignores it. *Washington Post.* Retrieved from http://voices.washingtonpost.com/answer-sheet/diane-ravitch/ravitch-merit-pays-long-unsucc.html

Stutz, T. (2011, June 23). Texas merit pay plan for teachers among programs slashed by Legislature. *Dallas Morning News.* Retrieved from http://www.dallasnews.com/news/politics/texas-legislature/headlines/20110623-texas-merit-pay-plan-for-teachers-among-programs-slashed-by-legislature-.ece

Troen, V., & Boles, K. C. (2005, September 28). How "merit pay" squelches teaching. *Boston Globe.* Retrieved from http://www.boston.com/news/education/k_12/articles/2005/09/28/how_merit_pay_squelches_teaching/

Wilson, S., Floden, R., & Ferrini-Mundy, J. (2001, February). *Teacher preparation research: Current knowledge, gaps, and recommendations.* Seattle: Center for the Study of Teaching and Policy, University of Washington. Retrieved from http://depts.washington.edu/ctpmail/PDFs/TeacherPrep-WFFM-02-2001.pdf

Winters, M., Ritter, G., Barnett, J., & Greene, J. (2008). *An evaluation of teacher performance pay in Arkansas.* Chicago: Heartland Institute. Retrieved from http://heartland.org/sites/all/modules/custom/heartland_migration/files/pdfs/20771.pdf

Winters, M. A., Ritter, G. W., Greene, J. P., & Marsh, R. (2009). Student outcomes and teacher productivity and perceptions in Arkansas. In M. G. Springer (Ed.), *Performance incentives: Their growing impact on American K–12 education* (pp. 273–293). Washington, DC: Brookings Institution Press.

Index

CORWIN

A SAGE Company

The Corwin logo—a raven striding across an open book—represents the union of courage and learning. Corwin is committed to improving education for all learners by publishing books and other professional development resources for those serving the field of PreK–12 education. By providing practical, hands-on materials, Corwin continues to carry out the promise of its motto: **"Helping Educators Do Their Work Better."**